What to Do When Love Turns Violent

What to Do When Love Turns Violent

A PRACTICAL

RESOURCE

FOR WOMEN

IN ABUSIVE

RELATIONSHIPS

Marian Betancourt

HarperPerennial

A Division of HarperCollinsPublishers

HarperCollins books may be purchased for educational, business, or sales promotional use. For information please write: Special Markets Department, HarperCollins Publishers, Inc., 10 East 53rd Street, New York, NY 10022.

FIRST EDITION

Designed by Alma Hochhauser Orenstein

Library of Congress Cataloging-in-Publication Data

Betancourt, Marian.
    What to do when love turns violent : a practical resource
for women in abusive relationships / Marian Betancourt
    p. cm.
    ISBN 0–06–273456–3
    1. Abused women—United States—Life skills guides.
2. Abused women—Counseling of—United States. 3. Abused
women—Services for—United States I. Title
HV6626.2.B47 1997   97–1710
362.82'928—dc21   CIP

97 98 99 00 01 ❖/RRD 10 9 8 7 6 5 4 3 2 1

PERMISSIONS

Barbara Hart, Legal Director, Pennsylvania Coalition Against Domestic Violence. Permission to quote from *Safety Planning for Children: Strategizing for Unsupervised Visitation with Batterers.*

*This book is dedicated to the hope that
one day we can all live and love without violence.*

*It is further dedicated to the people across the nation
who are committed to changing
our society's response to domestic violence.*

*And, as always,
it is for my children and my grandchildren.*

CONTENTS

ACKNOWLEDGMENTS

Many people gave generously and enthusiastically of their time and expertise because they believe in the need for this book. It is impossible to acknowledge each one, but I especially want to thank Deirdre Bialo-Padin, the former first deputy bureau chief, Domestic Violence Bureau of the Brooklyn district attorney's office in New York City; the domestic relations attorney Rose Ann Branda; the domestic violence police officer Linda Lepore and Detective Connie Turno of the 68th Precinct, NYPD; Barbara Anselmo of Victim Services; Edmund Stubbing, director, Police Programs, Victim Services, and his staff.

In addition, for sharing their knowledge and locating information for my research, I want to thank all of the state domestic violence coalitions. Thanks also to Bonnie J. Campell's staff at the Violence Against

Women Office of the U.S. Department of Justice; the AARP Women's Initiative; Debra Seeley Romero of the New Mexico Domestic Violence Legal HELPline; Mary Jane Friscia; and Cathy Colette of the American Federation of State, County, and Municipal Employees. Also, thanks to the Commonwealth Fund Commission on Women's Health.

INTRODUCTION

Now that the law has acknowledged that a man's violence against his wife or lover is a criminal act rather than a private matter, the response to women in abusive relationships is beginning to change. The police, the courts, hospitals, and the workplace can all provide help for women who need it. And while the response to domestic violence varies from one community to the next, all states and municipalities have networks of domestic violence advocates who can help you.

We still read news stories daily about women killed by former lovers or husbands despite having protective orders from the courts. But who was watching out for these women while the men were free on bail? Were there networks of people who knew how to protect her? How does a dangerous man walk into an office and kill his wife without arousing suspicion of the hundred other employees in the office? Did these women have safety plans to defend themselves? We cannot do it alone. We must tell people about the abuse and ask for help.

What to Do When Love Turns Violent is a nuts-and-bolts book for women who want to know how to protect themselves and get away from the violence as safely as possible. In this book you can find out how to seek protection through law enforcement and the justice system, how the health care system can help, and where to go with questions. It will give you information to help you make the right choices.

Women of all backgrounds and ages are hurt by domestic violence despite the misconception that it affects only poor and uneducated women. A study of police responses revealed that there were just as many domestic disturbance calls to police in Montgomery County, Maryland—a mostly white, upper-class suburb of Washington, D.C.—as there were in the same period in Harlem—a poor, mostly minority area of New York City.

In a northeastern middle-class neighborhood, a woman drove up to the police station in her Mercedes wearing only her nightgown. She was covered with blood because her husband, a prominent physician, had beaten her up with a tennis racket to such an extent that he had broken her nose, knocked out several teeth, blackened her eyes, punctured an eardrum, and broken her arm. The women was finally able to run from the house and drive to the police station.

Older women, too, are thought to be safe from domestic violence. Nothing could be further from the truth. In Massachusetts in the first half of 1995, five women over fifty were killed by spouses, and in 1994 the average age of battered women over sixty assaulted by their intimate partners in that state was seventy-seven. In Florida, a state with a large population of retirees, the governor's task force on domestic violence found that 71 percent of elderly victims of domestic violence crimes are abused by a spouse or intimate partner.

Some women find that once their husbands are retired, no longer able to vent their aggressions on the job or elsewhere, they become violent in the home. This late onset of violence is not unusual. In the summer of 1996, for example, an eighty-one-year-old actor who played a lovable old codger in a popular TV series was arrested in California for beating up his wife after an argument at a party. His wife was seventy-seven.

This book also tries to address the special problems of women in rural areas, where the danger from domestic violence is magnified by isolation and lack of transportation. The Rural Task Force of the National Coalition Against Domestic Violence found that in areas with small populations, where everybody knows everybody, people were less willing to call for help because the sheriff just might be the abusive man's brother. The Task Force is developing ways to help women in rural areas.

Most of the domestic violence in this country is perpetrated by men, and we use the word "he" throughout the book when talking about the abuser. While the woman is the violent partner in a tiny percentage of relationships (including lesbian relationships), it would be confusing and awkward to use the words "he or she" throughout the text.

The suggestions and ideas in this book are meant as a guide, and you must always evaluate your own situation and find out exactly what help is available where you are. But wherever you are, there is help. Just make that first call.

PREFACE

I have a distant memory. I am sitting up in my bed calling out to my mother, "Don't hit daddy." I say this over and over. I am three years old, but I fear for my mother's life if she hits my father back. He has been drinking and has been hitting her. Years later my mother told me how hurt she was because she believed I wanted to protect my father from any possible blows from her. I was never able to convince her to the contrary, that it was my fear for her safety that prompted the remark. But this is hazy recollection, layered with years. I remember the fear, not the details.

My father was an intelligent, upwardly mobile middle manager. He and my mother were the yuppies of their day, striving for the good life. My father was also an alcoholic. When I was five, he left my mother and me to marry another woman. My mother and I had a hardscrabble life after that. She, devastated by the broken dream, became chronically ill, physically and emotionally, and I grew up wanting—more than anything—to have someone to love.

So I got married as soon as I could, to have babies. It was an era somewhere between Elvis and the Beatles. My husband, eleven years my senior, seemed so settled, so steady. He had a good job and lived in a row house his father owned. I had babies, and I loved them (still do), but I did not rest. Because my husband was frequently laid off and working in a dying trade, I worked at whatever jobs I could get in the days before day care and househusbands. My husband's solution to unemployment was to hang out in the local bar rather than learn another trade.

Drinking often prompted the violence, but there were certainly times when he was sober. I know he loved me, and sometimes he was able to say it or show it, but the violence is what defined our relationship. And the violence is what I remember. This is not a distant memory. It's very close. I remember every detail.

The first time, I was beaten for refusing to cook something the way he liked it. Another time, I was beaten for having a minor accident with the car. Once I was beaten for challenging his "order" for me to take the children to Sunday school, even though he was the one who claimed to have religious faith. By this time my frustration level in trying to communicate was well into the danger zone. I said, "Fuck Sunday school"; then I tried to cover my face with my arms as he dragged me off the couch, tossed me onto the floor, and proceeded to kick me (he always wore steel-toed work shoes) toward the stairs. I was able to grab the door frame to slow the momentum of my body bouncing down a flight of stairs.

It was this incident that finally sent me out of the house in search of safety. Forced to leave without my sleeping children, aged two and four, I went to a neighbor's house, and her husband (a man half the size of my husband) immediately got out of bed, pulled on his pants, and started for the door to "straighten this guy out." My friend and I held him back because he might have been killed if he had interfered. Once again, the flashback to distant memory, begging my mother not to fight back.

After an hour I gathered my courage and went back. I had to. I could not leave my children. I did not have the money to go anyplace, even though I had been working to support us. In the years of violence, I never once considered that I might be able to find shelter somewhere or have him arrested. But when I went inside that house again, I did warn him that if he did it again, I would call the police. He shrugged. It made no difference to him. Most of the people around us—friends and family—considered domestic violence a private thing. They did not want to know. They avoided looking at the black-and-blue welts up and down my arms and around my neck.

I began secretly saving some money from each paycheck and opened my own bank account. I went to the library to research divorce. It took me three years to get out, to find a secure job and a place I could afford to live, and provide care for my children. During those three years my husband continued to threaten and abuse me. One afternoon, while he lingered at a neighborhood bar, I stole away with my children and a suitcase.

He demanded that I bring his children back or he would not support them. He stalked the home I now shared with another woman and her three children. (We worked rotating shifts, so one of us was always home with five children.) He stood outside at night watching, making sure I would not go out with another man. Was he out there with a gun? I did not feel safe leaving my house. He had often bragged threateningly about his hidden guns. Many years later my son confirmed that he indeed had at least two guns hidden in the basement.

Eventually he ceased stalking. But then I faced another three years of frustration with the justice system. Domestic violence gave me grounds for divorce in New York State, but because I wanted alimony, child support, and my belongings—which were still in the house—the justice system became impatient with me. My lawyer said, "You can't win every case."

During preliminary hearings, my ex-husband admitted to the beatings, and one court official said, "You know you should not do that." It was a mere slap on the hand, a "naughty, naughty," rebuke. No one—from police to lawyers to judges—ever suggested he get some psychological help, that he might have a serious problem, that it was a crime to assault your spouse, just as it is a crime to assault a stranger on the street.

Times have not changed a hell of a lot. But we have made some progress. There is help out there now, and with this book I mean to help you find it.

DISCLAIMER

This book is meant to educate women about the resources available to help them be safe if they are or were in relationships with abusive men. There is help available in every state and city, but naturally some communities are more responsive and better organized than others. This book offers suggestions, not solutions. Before you take any action, evaluate your safety and talk with your local domestic violence advocates. They are there to help you.

CHAPTER 1

How the Police Can Help You

Reporting domestic violence to police appears to reduce the risk of a husband attacking his wife again by as much as 62 percent.

NATIONAL CRIME VICTIMIZATION SURVEY

Domestic violence is a federal crime. As new laws are more consistently applied, this fact will sink into society's consciousness, although it may take a bit longer before men shake the belief that they are entitled to push women around and get away with it. Nevertheless, the law is now on our side, and there is an ever-widening network of help available: police, courts, hospitals, and domestic violence shelters. For most women the way into that network begins with the police. Calling 911 sets the criminal justice system in motion when you are assaulted, terrorized, or stalked by your abusive intimate partner.

Emerging Police Protocols

As a result of the 1994 federal anticrime bill, which included the Violence Against Women Act, most police and sheriff's departments now have written protocols for domestic violence. Law-enforcement officers are required to keep you safe if you are being abused by your intimate partner and to act as liaisons in a network of interventions to help you get away from the abuse. And now in most states they must arrest your abusive partner.

If police fail to keep you safe, they are liable. This liability grew out of a class-action suit in California in 1977 in which three female attorneys sued the Oakland Police Department and the city of Oakland on behalf of women abused by violent men. This suit, the first in the domestic violence movement, resulted in new police procedures, police training, and city funding for local domestic violence shelters. In 1985 a woman in Torrington, Connecticut, won a $2-million settlement from the city for failure of the police department to protect her from her husband's violence. This case, the first tried in federal court, was a catalyst in Connecticut's passage of the 1986 Family Violence and Response Act, which now mandates arrest in domestic violence cases when probable cause exists.

The 1994 Violence Against Women Act resulted from years of persistent lobbying by women's groups. Its passage created Justice Department funding to local communities to train the police and the courts in the realities of domestic violence, and to coordinate efforts to help women to safety. It also provided for the national domestic violence hot line, launched in 1996, so that a woman anywhere in the United States can be connected to the resources she needs to get away from a violent partner.

A New Police Sensitivity

Federal funds have helped develop domestic violence protocols in about half the nation's police departments and sheriff's offices. In large metropolitan areas, police department specialists in community affairs and crime prevention have been joined by domestic violence officers, whose job is to help you get the social and human services you need. However, in some communities these officers are not always on duty at night or on weekends, when many domestic violence incidents take place. (Sunday night is the most common time for domestic violence according to a study of their state by the New Jersey Coalition for Battered Women.)

In many communities where police have taken domestic violence seriously, their response has generally been applauded. In their first year of operation—with the help of federal grants—the Domestic Violence Unit of the Metro Nashville Police Department investigated eighteen thousand domestic violence calls and reduced Nashville's domestic homicide rate by 71 percent. In the New York City Police Department, a domestic violence police program began in 1983, but it was not until 1994—eleven years later—that all precincts were required to have a domestic violence officer. Whether or not there are domestic violence specialists in your community, all officers must follow the new rules.

In rural areas the reality may be different. While police may be just as concerned and cooperative, their availability might be limited by the great distances and isolation. You might be served by a single county sheriff or deputy, or have to rely on state police. If you live in a remote corner of a district with only one officer and another crime is happening at the same time, you may never get emergency help when you need it. It is therefore essential to develop a safety plan and be connected to a network of advocates who can help.

What to Tell the Police When You Call

If you are in immediate danger, always call 911 and try to give as much information as you can. The more the police know before they arrive, the more effective they will be. In a handful of communities, the police dispatcher can run a computer background check immediately in order to let the responding officers know whether there have been similar calls to your address in the past, if an order of protection is in effect, or if a gun is registered to anyone. Although police computer networks are improving—in Hawaii there is a model plan to have computers in the police cars—most background checking goes through channels at the police station or the state capital or a central registry during normal business hours.

Most of this information is determined later, after the police have filed a report at the station house, so the more information you can provide, the better they can help you.

Try to tell them

- if you and your abuser are at the same location
- if you are being threatened with a weapon
- if there are children present
- if the assault is still in progress
- if a protective order exists
- if anyone has been using drugs or drinking
- how badly you or anyone else is injured
- if you are disabled

In most emergencies you won't have enough time to remember all this, but the more information the radio dispatcher is able to give to the police in the street, the more efficient the response will be. For example, if police know your abusive partner has a gun, they might call for backup, or they will come without sirens so they can catch the man off guard. In some jurisdictions police are instructed to approach *all* domestic violence calls silently. Many officers do not park directly in front of the house.

This caution is necessary to avoid provoking the assailant, who might take you hostage or kill you, and to protect officers as well. Domestic violence calls are the fifth most dangerous police assignments. In 1996 a young police officer was killed in New York City when he was shoved into a broken mirror by an enraged man who had been beating up his common-law wife. A police lieutenant was shot and killed when he went to the aid of a woman who was being stalked by a former boyfriend.

If you are being assaulted and yanked away from the phone, try to leave it off the hook, and keep talking or screaming so police can trace the call and find you. The priority police give to your call depends on the degree of immediate danger conveyed in your call as well as what else is going on in their district at the time. If there are two armed robberies in progress, the police response to your call might not be as fast; but in areas with a substantial police force, somebody will come. In many cities domestic violence calls receive the second-highest priority after calls to assist an officer in trouble.

Never put yourself in greater danger than already exists. If you can remain where you are until police arrive, then you will be able to explain what happened. If, however, you need to leave the scene to protect yourself, then do so. If you are gone when police arrive they will talk to your abusive partner, who is likely to tell them nothing is wrong. They will make a report anyway, because there was a call about violence.

If You Are Not a Citizen

If you are a lawful permanent resident or possess a valid visa, you have the same rights as anyone else; new immigration laws mean you cannot be deported for calling the police to report domestic abuse. You are still entitled to help from the police and safety from the violence. You can go to a shelter and also get a temporary restraining order against your abuser.

In 1996 the Immigration and Naturalization Service ruled that abused spouses and children of legal residents can petition for legal status on their own, so you need not choose between abuse and deportation. Some communities, like Albuquerque, New Mexico, with a large immigrant population, have created special domestic violence programs, such as the Albuquerque Border City Project, to facilitate response to immigrant women.

The changes in the federal welfare laws in 1996 may restrict the services available to immigrants—legal and illegal—but police and hospital emergency rooms cannot turn you away in an emergency.

If you do not speak English, police can get an

interpreter, either from their own ranks or from the community. In some cities a call to 911 or the AT&T Language Line can connect you and the police to a translator.

What the Police Will Do

When the police arrive, go into another room with the officers so you can speak without being shouted down or interrupted. Try to tell them what happened and ignore any taunts from your abusive partner. He knows he can be arrested and might try to appear rational and calm so he can talk his way out of an arrest. Though your home might be filled with broken furniture and shattered glass, though you might be crying and terrified, he will point to you and say, "Look at her, she's the one who's out of control." If your injuries are not visible, he may even deny attacking you. If you are obviously injured, he may claim that you hit him first and that he had to defend himself, or that it was your fault. "She made me do it. She insulted my manhood." Try not to respond to this lame excuse of the chronic abuser. There *is* no excuse. You are not responsible for his violence. He is. The evidence at the scene speaks for itself. The fact that you—or someone—called and said you were being attacked is all you need.

Describe the violence as accurately as you can. Give them a blow-by-blow account of what happened. Officers at the scene may also interview children, other family members, and neighbors who might have seen or heard the violence.

If your violent partner has fled by the time police arrive, the police will have to go find him. This can be done immediately or after a warrant has been issued for his arrest. Police will need your help in finding and identifying him. Give them addresses of friends and relatives, known hangouts, his workplace, car license plate number, and a photo.

GETTING TO A SAFE PLACE

If police do not take away your abusive partner, they can take you away after they wait while you collect your belongings such as clothes, important papers, medications, money, and the evidence of domestic violence. They can take you to the home of a friend or relative in the area, or to the police station where they can help you locate the nearest family violence shelter. Because shelters are so crowded, they may have to take you to your community's emergency shelter.

If police take away your abuser, they might be able to offer you help in getting your locks changed and obtaining an emergency protective order while the abusive man is in custody. Ask them to let you call your local or national domestic violence hot line. If your police department has domestic violence officers, they will be able to give you more information.

GOING TO A HOSPITAL

If you are injured or in shock, police should call for an ambulance or take you to a hospital emergency room, or to your own physician or clinic if that is an option. Hospitals are also operating under new rules about domestic violence, and if they do not help you, they can lose their accreditation.

Never refuse medical attention. It is imperative to seek an objective medical opinion and evaluation. Many bruises and fractures are not always apparent right away. Injuries could swell and discolor later. If you have dark skin, discoloration may not be noticeable until hours later, or when swelling begins. You could be unaware of internal bleeding or contusions that will cause problems later. A physician can examine you for deeper injuries, as well as signs of long-term abuse, and make a diagnosis for treatment as well as a medical report you can use as evidence in getting a protective order or following up on criminal charges.

If you are pregnant, let police know right away. Nearly half of all women who are beaten up by intimate partners are pregnant. Any kind of trauma can harm your baby. More babies are born with birth defects as a result of domestic violence than a combination of all diseases and illnesses for which we now immunize pregnant women. An abused mother is two times more likely to miscarry and four times more likely to have a low-birth-weight baby.

In chapter 5 you will find more information about getting medical care and how hospitals can help you as another intervention resource.

CONFISCATION OF WEAPONS

Police will also remove any weapons or potentially harmful instruments like baseball bats if they believe they were used to assault you, even if no arrest is made. Weapons are used in 30 percent of domestic violence incidents, according to the Bureau of Justice Statistics, and of these weapons, 40 percent are knives or sharp instruments, 34 percent guns, 12 percent blunt objects, and 15 percent other weapons. A weapon includes not only a gun or knife, but also objects used as weapons, such as a piece of furniture, a lamp, ropes, or chains.

If you have a protective order against your abusive partner, federal law now prohibits him from possessing firearms or ammunition. The only exception to this is if he is an on-duty law enforcement officer himself or a member of the military.

GATHERING EVIDENCE

Never clean up the house right after an assault. Unfortunately, many women do this because they want to erase all memory of the violence. (Men do it to hide the evidence.) But in doing this, you get rid of pieces of broken glass, torn and bloody clothing, clumps of hair pulled from your head, and broken furniture pieces used as weapons. This is all potentially important evidence and should be collected in a plastic bag, labeled, and taken away by the police to store in their property room.

The importance of identifying and collecting evidence of domestic violence cannot be overemphasized. Many women who have gone to court to get a restraining order, to testify in the abuser's arrest, or to get custody of their children have failed because it came down to their word against his. After years of living with control and intimidation, you may not be able to be objective and remember everything when you speak to a judge. But if you have hard evidence, it does not matter. Even if your abuser has a good attorney or the court is not sympathetic to you, the evidence speaks for itself.

What happened to you is a crime, and where it happened is a crime scene. Police have traditionally been more thorough at searching the scene for evidence when the offender was a stranger. Remind them that this is a crime scene and should be treated like one. The more evidence you collect, the more help you can get for yourself to build a safer life. Good evidence will make it easier to get a protective order, financial help, stronger punishment for the abuser, and tougher penalties if he does not stay away from you.

Police officers should be looking for all evidence of harm or injury to you, such as

- torn or bloody clothing
- damage to furniture, walls, windows, a car, or other property
- broken objects used as weapons
- signs of break-in through a window, door, or garage
- threatening messages on your answering machine
- letters or written messages containing threats
- your own records, diaries, letters, and reports from police, courts, hospitals
- names and phone numbers of witnesses
- photos of you showing cuts, bruises, black eyes, or other signs of physical injury

PHOTOGRAPHING YOUR INJURIES

If a picture is worth a thousand words, then photographs of your injuries and any damage to your home are critical evidence. In Wailuku, Hawaii, as part of a domestic violence program, police officers carry cameras in their cars in order to take pictures at the crime scene. This may be the case in other jurisdictions as well, but in general don't expect the police to have a camera with them. Despite donations of special instant cameras to some law enforcement agencies from the Polaroid Corporation, the film is so expensive that most police do not routinely have access to this technology. They may not get photographs unless they take you to the station house and borrow a camera from the detective division.

If you can afford it, buy a camera and always keep film on hand for just this reason. You could need it at any time. Ask the police to use your camera or ask a neighbor or friend with a camera to take the pictures. Ask them to photograph your injuries as well as damage to the surroundings, such as blood on the wall or broken furniture, which can be used as evidence in a criminal or civil case hearing and in seeking a petition for a protective order. If you have a neighbor or friend with a video camera, have him or her make a video of you, preferably at the scene, while you describe what happened.

Remember to take pictures soon after the assault— by the next day, if possible, because many bruises will not show up immediately. For example, if you were punched in the eye, it may not turn black and blue for several hours. Have photographs developed where the date is stamped on the print. In the weeks and months that follow the violence, your memories of the event may fade, but the images in the photographs and on videotape will be there forever.

THE DETAILED POLICE REPORT

Police are required to complete a report every time they respond to a domestic violence call. Whether your violent partner is arrested or not, this report is the official record of what happened to you, and you will need this report in the future. Take your time to be sure police include all the information you give them. Be sure they listen to you and write down what you say as well as what they saw. Most cops hate paperwork. If they enjoyed filling out forms they would have become accountants. They should take note of your emotional state at the time and describe and document your injuries and the past abuse you tell them about. They should also describe the crime scene, interview other witnesses, and get a statement from the abuser, noting his exact words, his emotional state, and any comments he makes to them.

What you say counts as evidence, so the statement you give the police is very important. Tell them to write down direct quotes of what your abuser said while hurting you, such as "I'll kill you if you do that again," or "I told you I didn't want you to wear that dress." The well-documented report should tell the story of the violence to everyone who will later read it, including domestic violence police officers and advocates, lawyers, and judges. These people are often busy and pressured and may read dozens of reports per day. If your case is hard to comprehend or not compelling enough, you could be at a disadvantage.

This is the official record of what happened to you. This report is vital even without an arrest for the following reasons:

- You can use it to substantiate your story if you do decide to press charges later.
- As documented history, it gets you faster response from police and courts when the violence recurs.
- If he is arrested, it may help set a higher bail, so he can remain locked up longer.
- It can be used to show good cause for the court to grant a protective order.
- It can help the prosecutor win your case in court without you having to testify.
- It is an important legal document in any proceedings for divorce or child custody.

Read the report carefully before you sign it; if anything is incorrect, ask the officers to change it. Police are not hired for their skills as reporters or writers, so ask them to change anything that is not detailed enough, seems misleading, or does not seem accurate or complete.

Keep in mind that you can add to the report later. When you have calmed down, you may remember other important details. You can attach photographs, medical reports, court records, and statements from witnesses. Some police departments assign many numbers to their reports: a complaint number, a report number, a case number, a docket number. Find out what numbers you need to know.

Don't forget to get the name and badge numbers of the police officers.

What Else Your Police Report Will Do

Until recently, few states collected enough information to indicate how many crimes were committed against women. Assault between husband and wife was not distinguished from crimes by unknown assailants. Only seventeen states kept data on reported domestic violence, and then only if it involved murder, rape, or serious bodily injury. Now law enforcement agencies in most states maintain a record of domestic abuse incidents. This information may go to a central domestic violence bureau in the state, the Federal Bureau of Investigation, or the Department of Justice. It will become part of a much larger effort to discover just how much domestic violence occurs in this country. This reporting helps all the agencies involved to protect women from violence.

If a stranger beat you up, you would not hesitate to report the crime to the police, yet most women do not report domestic violence to police. According to a National Crime Victimization Survey, six times as many women are hurt by their husbands and lovers as are hurt by strangers. And most do not report the violence to police, largely because they fear reprisals from their abuser. But without intervention, violence only continues; in a third of the cases, it leads to homicide.

Stronger police action can help to protect women, and it can make some men think twice about using violence. It sends an important message that they cannot get away with the abuse, that they will be held accountable for their actions.

In the next chapter you will find information about how to be safe if your abusive partner is arrested.

CONNECTING WITH A DOMESTIC VIOLENCE ADVOCATE

Police should be able to connect you with your local domestic violence network, which may be a shelter system, women's center, or victim services agency. In many cities a social service agency such as New York's Victim Services Agency works directly with police. This collaboration allows the social service agency to provide you with shelter and other emergency resources with police protection. The police often do not know where the shelters are because the locations are confidential. Call the state or federal hot line while the police are with you, and ask for referrals to services in your area.

BEFORE THE POLICE LEAVE

If you choose to stay in the house, don't let the police leave until they have explained what you should do to be safe and until you have talked with a domestic violence network or crisis line for information and advice.

Ask the police what you have a right to do, and also ask about the probable results of those actions. It is very important that you know how safe you will be if they take your abusive partner away and arrest him. Asking the following questions might prove useful:

- Will he be released before the end of the day or night?
- How will they keep him away from you if he becomes even more enraged and violent?
- Would it be best if you left?
- Can they keep him in custody until you have the locks changed? (In some cities the police or district attorney can help you get new locks free of charge. There is more about such resources in chapter 3.)

CHAPTER 2

How to Be Safe if He Is Arrested

*Some law enforcement officials believe the reason
the national murder rate declined 40 percent in the
mid-1990s is that men who beat up their wives and
girlfriends are now being arrested.*

In the past, when two police officers responded to a domestic dispute call, one officer would walk the man around and cool him off while the other would ask the woman if she wanted to file a complaint, hoping she did not. Arrests were rarely made because domestic violence was considered a private matter best addressed through mediation. But this kind of irresolute police intervention does nothing to curb the violence that, left unchecked, can lead to homicide.

It was not until 1988 that all fifty states finally had laws to provide civil and criminal remedies for women in violent relationships. In 1977 Oregon became the first state to require arrest for domestic violence; by

1996, twenty-seven states and the District of Columbia had adopted mandatory arrest. This means police must arrest your abusive partner if he assaults you. The officer does not have to witness the assault. He or she only needs reason to believe it happened.

While some studies show that mandatory arrest does seem to make men stop and think before getting violent, opinions vary about whether mandatory arrest is an immediate deterrent in all cases. In the long term women will be safer if society makes men understand they are being held accountable for their violence against women.

What Mandatory Arrest Means

The rules about domestic violence are constantly changing, and in states where arrest is not yet mandatory, arrest is "preferred" or "strongly recommended," which means police must take it seriously because it is now a federal crime. While all states have their own definitions of such laws, the stronger mandatory laws mean that the phrase "may arrest" is changed to "shall arrest." A police officer can arrest when there is probable cause that an abuser has committed an assault resulting in bodily injury to another person and there is danger of further violence. All states have their own domestic violence laws, and the degrees and definitions are not the same everywhere, even for mandatory arrest.

Mandatory arrest is most effective when it is part of a coordinated and integrated criminal justice response to domestic violence with consistent follow-through by domestic violence advocates, victim services providers, prosecutors, and judges. Mandatory arrest sets justice in motion. Minneapolis police, for example, report each domestic assault arrest to the Domestic Abuse Intervention Project by phone, allowing the abused woman to get more timely help. In Nevada anyone arrested under this mandatory statute will not be able to bail out for at least twelve hours so that the abused woman will have time to leave, seek help, or otherwise ensure her safety.

If you live in a state with a mandatory arrest policy, police will take your abusive partner away, and the arrest is out of your hands. He is charged with a crime against the state, just as if he had assaulted a stranger on the street. If he is not on the scene when police arrive, they will issue a warrant for his arrest and go find him.

If you live on one of the five hundred Native American reservations in the United States, tribal law takes precedence over state laws, which are sometimes different. If you live off the reservation, then you are subject to state law. Federal law supersedes state and tribal law, so the violence is still a federal crime. Here's an example of a potential problem: let's say you are dating a man who lives on a reservation, but you live off the reservation in a nearby town. If the man assaults you in your home and then flees back to the reservation, he cannot be arrested by the town police. The same applies to military bases. Local police cannot go onto a base to apprehend an abusive man. They can, however, ask the military police to cooperate in seeking justice.

Misdemeanors and Felonies

It is important for you to know what your abuser will be charged with and what those charges mean to your future safety. Crimes are either misdemeanors or felonies, two different categories which carry different penalties. Felonies are generally treated more seriously than misdemeanors. If he punches you, it could be a misdemeanor, but if he hits you with a weapon, it is a felony. This generally means anything used as a weapon, even a shoe.

Keep in mind that in some states and counties, definitions of these crimes may differ and that a crime can move from classification as a misdemeanor to a felony with more evidence if your abuser has been similarly charged before. In many states this will happen if your abuser has two previous domestic violence misdemeanors. In Rhode Island convicted second-time offenders must now spend at least ten days in jail. In some states the third offense is automatically a felony.

Assault, sometimes called battery, is a misdemeanor. Assault is when he causes visible injury or substantial pain by hitting or kicking you. Misdemeanors usually require less than a year in jail and smaller fines. Many people found guilty of a misdemeanor will not spend any time in jail.

A felony assault is an attack or attempted attack with a weapon that results in serious injury such as broken bones, loss of teeth, loss of consciousness, and requires two or more days of hospitalization. Felonies can be punishable with at least a year in jail and large fines if a conviction is made.

Harassment can involve physical contact, like shoving or pushing, that does not result in physical injury. Threatening phone calls and letters fall into this category.

Menacing with a weapon is when he waves a gun at you and threatens you. For example, he tells you, "One of these days, I'll kill you." This is a misdemeanor and you can file a complaint with the police.

Criminal mischief means damaging property: breaking down your door or slashing your tires, for example.

He can be charged with breaking and entering or burglary if he forcibly enters your home when you are legally separated or divorced, especially if you have an order of protection forbidding him to do this. If he breaks in to steal documents or cash when you are not home, he can be charged with burglary.

Stalking is when your abuser repeatedly follows you, harasses you, and threatens you. It may be considered a felony if this happens while there is an order of protection against him. Stalking is an extremely common crime of abusive men and is now a federal crime with tougher penalties. (See chapter 7 for more information about stalking.)

Violating a protective order can have tough penalties now that the federal law is behind it. But in most states violating a protective order is a misdemeanor charge of "contempt of court." In a few states, like New York, it is contempt in the first degree and therefore a felony. If the order forbids him to come to your home and he breaks in and attacks you, he can be arrested not only for contempt of court, but also for breaking and entering or assault. In some states a second offense against a restraining order is an automatic felony.

With a misdemeanor arrest, the offender may be locked up from twelve to thirty-six hours, often enough time for you to move out of the home or have the locks changed and get an emergency order of protection (see chapter 4). With a felony arrest he may be away longer, depending on whether he can make bail. The next chapter describes the process of prosecuting him for his crimes.

Question the police about changes in the laws so you can stay as well informed as possible.

Your Risk of Being Arrested for Defending Yourself

If you hit your abusive partner in self-defense, he will likely accuse you of assaulting him, and it is possible that you could be arrested, too. If you hit him back with a weapon such as a lamp, you may be charged with felonious assault, while he might be charged with simple assault, a misdemeanor, because he did not use a weapon—even though he's twice as big as you. Police at the scene must decide who is the primary physical aggressor, but be aware that mandatory arrest laws have resulted in more double arrests in some communities.

If you are arrested, ask immediately for your domestic violence hot line and tell them what happened. There is a wide legal network available to assist women who are charged with crimes against their abusive partners. Keep in mind that women are often more seriously punished for using force to defend themselves because of society's old but still lingering belief that a man has a right to abuse his wife but that she does not have the right to fight back.

Making a Citizen's Arrest

In many states, if the police do not have a mandatory arrest policy, or if you believe they did not pay enough attention to the facts and evidence you know exists, you can file a criminal complaint and make a citizen's arrest.

Without a mandatory arrest policy, some police might be reluctant to arrest your abusive partner. They may suspect that you will not follow through if an arrest is made. Or they may want to protect you from additional danger from your abusive partner if an arrest is made. They know that abusive men who believe they have lost control are at their most dangerous and will retaliate. If he is taken away by police, he has lost control.

Foremost in your mind is whether or not having him arrested will help keep you safe or whether it will further inflame his violence when he is released from court, often within a few hours of the arrest. Ask police the following questions:

- How long is he likely to be in jail?
- What is your role in the follow-up process?
- Will you be notified when he is released?
- How can you be safe when he is released?

If you decide you want him arrested, the police will give you the appropriate forms to fill out; once you have signed the papers, they are required to take the offender into custody. This can also be done from a hospital bed or from another location to which you have fled. (Be aware that your partner may also try to make a citizen's arrest by charging you with abuse, and you may both be taken into custody.) The complaint you file goes to the district attorney or judge, and an arrest warrant is issued.

You can also file the complaint later or the next day. If you did not call the police when your partner assaulted you but later decide that you want him arrested, go to the police department or the county or state prosecuting attorney's (district attorney) office. Tell them you were the victim of a crime and you want to file a report about it. The police or prosecutor must listen to what you have to say and take down the information you give. Tell them everything your abusive partner did, and bring as much evidence as possible: medical records, photographs, and other items mentioned in the previous chapter. Bring a photo of your abusive partner, names and addresses of his friends and relatives, his job location, and his driver's license and registration numbers so they can find him and arrest him.

In such a case, you should be willing to follow through with the charges and be prepared to cope with a series of interviews, take time off from work, and possibly testify in court—in front of your abusive partner, his attorney, and many strangers. However, if the evidence is strong, it is possible that you will not have to appear in court. This process may take some time, and you may want to go to a shelter or to another safe place.

In states where there is no citizen's arrest, there is

a procedure for filing a complaint with the police or court. This can lead to police action or it can lead to a summons for the abuser to appear in court and face charges.

Deciding Why You Want Him Arrested

Although an abusive man obviously deserves to be arrested, be clear in your own mind why you want him arrested and how it will affect your safety. Some women hesitate to have someone they love arrested once the violence cools and he expresses remorse. Some women bow to family pressure. And many women simply do not have the resources to carry on alone if the abusive man is taken away and cannot go to work.

Evaluate the charges and the likely results after talking with domestic violence advocates and the police. Decide what you want to happen. Do you want him punished? Do you want revenge? Do you want him taken away or ordered into counseling? Do you want to stand up to him and let him know he cannot abuse you and get away with it? Do you want to reassure your children that you are taking steps to end the violence? When you make this decision, be prepared to follow through. Studies have shown that most women want their abusers kept away from them and punished, but many others want them used as an example. Many women follow through despite the fear, because now, more help is available.

The advantages of filing criminal charges are that upon conviction, he will have a criminal record. He can be fined or go to jail. This sends a message to all abusive men that their violence is a crime with serious penalties and cannot be tolerated.

On the other hand, you cannot control the processing of a criminal case. The prosecution may continue without you. A criminal case often drags out over a long period of time, especially if your abusive partner has a good attorney or appeals to the court.

It is very important for you to make up your own mind after you have all the information and have talked with appropriate people. It is likely that even if arrested, he might soon be out of jail, poised for revenge. And while in jail, even for a few days, he has access to a phone and can harass you, threaten you, or ask his friends to intervene. Some men spend jail time working out, building strength, or even reading up on domestic violence laws in the prison library. When he comes out, he could be stronger and more determined to beat you up—now with good reason, he tells himself, because you sent him to jail and shamed him in public.

Cooperating with the Police

Once an arrest is made, your case is investigated by a detective. In smaller towns and rural areas, this may be the same sheriff or deputy who made the arrest. The detective will get background history from you and evaluate the degree of danger you're in. Detectives will want evidence to make a case: photographs, weapons, tape-recorded conversations, medical records, and past history of abuse. They will evaluate the evidence, take photos of your injuries if that has not already been done, and talk with any other witnesses. The investigator might also want to put a tap on the phone lines in order to record any threats and harassment you receive from the abusive man.

If your abusive partner was not arrested at the scene of the last violent incident, but you press charges and detectives decide that there is enough evidence, they will make an arrest.

According to a police detective who is part of a round-the-clock pilot program on domestic violence, 95 percent of the men she must arrest come in voluntarily because she warns them that if they do not come in, she will go to their workplace and take them away in handcuffs. Most men do not want that to happen. This detective, who handles only domestic violence cases, has the highest number of arrests in her precinct, which means there are more arrests for domestic violence than any other crime in the neighborhood.

Once your partner is arrested, you will have to identify him. This can be done without any confrontation by viewing through a one-way glass, although this is a difficult and emotional time for many women.

If your partner is acting repentant, telling you he loves you and asking you how you could do this to him, you may waver in your decision to go forward and cooperate with police. (Some women want to kiss their abusive partner good-bye before police take him away.) He will promise that it will never happen again and that he will seek help for his violence or his drinking. He will beg you to drop the charges and stop cooperating with the police so that the case will be dismissed for lack of evidence. If this does not work, he will intimidate and pressure you and may become violent again.

A social worker who often counseled other women about domestic violence was in an abusive relationship herself—and at first failed to take her own advice—she avoided asking for help. One night when the man she lived with menaced her with a knife as he held their three-year-old daughter in his arms, she fled for her life and went to the police. When she calmed down, she did not want to arrest the man, but the police talked with her and asked her to think about what would happen to her child in such an environment. She agreed to press charges, and they brought in the man. With the help of domestic violence advocates and the police, the woman left town with her daughter that night. A few months later the detective got a letter from the woman saying that she now had her own apartment, had a good life, and that she had her self-respect back.

Detectives are being trained to deal with the changing emotions of women who, simultaneously loving and hating their abusive partners, sometimes blame the police for ruining their marriages. To one of these women a detective said, "Go look in the mirror, look at your black-and-blue breast, and tell me who is ruining your marriage." This detective believes she has every right to get women involved in cooperating with the case. Even if you're not working with such a sympathetic officer, express your fears and concerns and ask lots of questions. Make sure the police understand you are risking your life to do the right thing. (In the next chapter you will find out more about the process of arrest and prosecution and how it affects you.)

Some Good Reasons for Arresting Him

Consider some of the following points from the Domestic Abuse Intervention Project in Duluth, Minnesota:

- Assault is a crime in all fifty states. If you were assaulted by a stranger on the street, you would expect an arrest.
- Abusive men get violent because they get away with it, and they get what they want. It is time they learned some other way.
- If a man is abusive and there are no serious conse-

quences for his use of violence, his violent behavior is reinforced.

- The courts can place controls on a violent man that friends and family members cannot. They can send him to jail, levy heavy fines, restrict his bail, serve protective orders, and send him to a batterer's counseling program.

CHAPTER 3

How to Build a Strong Case for Justice and Safety

After three years of implementing domestic violence protocols, the San Francisco district attorney's office reported a 44 percent increase in the rate of convictions in felony cases.

In the past the burden of proof was usually on the woman as the chief witness against her abusive lover or husband; typically there was an absence or shortage of evidence collection and reports, and the violence was not treated like a crime. The woman herself was the only evidence. She was under enormous pressure, not only from her family urging her not to humiliate them in public, but also from an indifferent prosecutor and an unsympathetic judge and jury, who likely believed that she got what she asked for. So, while a woman put her life on the line and tried to buck a hostile system, her abusive partner was free on bail to intimidate, harass, and threaten to kill her if she testified against him.

Is it any surprise that once on the stand this woman might be reluctant to tell the real story of the violence inflicted upon her? It was safer to say, "Oh, it was my fault" or "It was all a misunderstanding." The jury took her word for it, without realizing how terrified this woman was. Many women have risked their lives by testifying against their abusers, only to come out no safer than they had been before. The violent men were still free to beat up or kill women who tried to bring them to justice for their crimes.

More and more prosecutors are realizing that if they *build a strong case on the evidence,* they need not put you in this dangerous position. After all, in murder cases criminals are prosecuted every day without testimony from the victim! With more attention being paid to domestic crimes, police are becoming more alert about gathering evidence, and prosecutors are often able to enhance a case against the abuser without having to bring you into court to testify. In a case with strong evidence, such as detailed police and medical reports, photographs of your injuries, and physical evidence such as torn and bloody clothing, they can often succeed without your testimony.

However, even with the proliferation of domestic violence services and the infusion of federal funds to train prosecuting attorneys about spousal abuse, many problems still contribute to a very low rate of prosecution of domestic violence cases. Misdemeanor cases are sometimes dismissed with no effort to find out if you're willing to cooperate and without any apparent concern for your safety. When your abusive partner is arrested and you are asked to cooperate with the prosecution, be certain the prosecutor understands your fear of retaliation by your abuser. Ask what will be done to keep you safe if you cooperate with their case. Ask for the protections outlined later in this chapter.

If a prosecutor urges you to testify without exploring the full impact on your safety, find a domestic violence advocate or a victim advocate and let him or her know your fears and concerns. While you can be subpoenaed by the court and ordered to testify under threat of a contempt charge yourself, you may be in more danger from your abuser, who may be out on bail, threatening you with more violence or taking away any means of support for you and possibly your children. In addition to the danger of retaliation, it is intimidating and embarrassing talking to a roomful of strangers about the intimate details of your life. You may still love your abuser and find it extremely difficult to accuse him publicly.

The purpose of making the system better is not to make your life worse. The ultimate goal is to keep you safe and to punish the criminal. New arrest laws and heightened awareness in the justice system show that some of this is changing and that more women are willing to go through the ordeal if the prosecutors and courts will protect them. Domestic violence bureaus have been established in some metropolitan district attorney's offices.

Cooperating with the Prosecution

Once your abusive partner has been arrested, there are a series of steps—which both of you take—through the criminal justice system as the case then proceeds from arraignment to either a settlement, a dismissal, or a trial. How long this takes and how you will be involved depends on the charges, the depth of the evidence, whether or not he pleads guilty, and how your community addresses domestic violence. Misdemeanors can generally be resolved in a month or two, while a felony can take up to a year or more if there is a trial.

If you are fortunate enough to live in a community with little tolerance for domestic violence or a community that has a domestic violence bureau in the district attorney's office, you will be able to work within a system designed to offer you as much protection as possible. Such bureaus exist in many communities in California, Washington, New York, Minnesota, Pennsylvania, and other states. In the domestic violence unit of the Kings County district attorney's office in Brooklyn, more than 7,000 cases are handled each year. At all times there are at least 1,500 cases pending among twenty assistant district attorneys. In a small town or rural area there may be only part-time county prosecutors and judges, and months or weeks may go by before your case can be heard.

If you live where there is no domestic violence bureau or where attitudes change slowly, you should get help from your domestic violence network. If you know what the system is capable of providing—as described later in this chapter—then you can strongly suggest it be provided to you.

Domestic Violence Advocates in the Courts

In some states domestic violence advocates or victim advocates work in the courts. Call your state domestic violence coalition and find out if they can help you in court; perhaps there is already such an advocate at the court. The New Jersey Coalition for Battered Women reports court assistance as their most requested service. Most states now legally allow you to bring a domestic violence or victim advocate to court with you. In Minnesota, a state with strong domestic violence laws, a court rule gives legal status to the role of the domestic violence advocate despite criticism commonly heard from attorneys that non-lawyers are practicing law. Since 1988 the Rhode Island Coalition Against Domestic Violence has had a statewide victim advocacy program with full-time advocates—both paid and volunteer—in all of the eight district courts. The coalition oversees all domestic violence cases in Rhode Island.

In some communities there are other agencies, such as victim or social service agencies or bar association committees, that can help you in the courtroom. An advocate can educate you in the prosecution process, let you know when your abusive partner will be released from custody, arrange for transportation or child care when you need to appear in court, make sure the system protects your safety, and offer moral support. Such advocates can also help you with any court business, such as petitioning for a protective order.

How the Court Can Protect You

In addition to punishment for crimes, the courts may offer a variety of remedies and protective measures. If these resources are not offered to you, ask for them. There is no reason why they cannot be provided. Here is a list of possibilities:

- a protective order making it illegal for him to come near you or harass you (see the next chapter for information on protective orders)
- a pendant alarm to wear or a cell phone to carry so you can alert the police if you are being stalked or in danger of being attacked
- relocation to a shelter, safe house, or hotel, through a witness protection program if necessary

- a traveler's aid program to provide bus or plane tickets
- intervention with immigration and victim services on your behalf
- cutting off your abusive partner's telephone access to you from prison
- notifying you when he is free on bail or released from jail
- helping you get food stamps and social services
- changing your locks free of charge

In an effort to protect women from further violence, the district attorney's domestic violence bureau in Brooklyn will arrange for a voice mail service where messages can be left so as not to risk a call to a woman's home. They also create a letterhead and mailing address without the official logo so they can contact women safely by mail without their abusers knowing they are in contact with the district attorney's office.

Not all communities are set up this well, but you can ask for these things! You have a right to be as safe as possible if you are asked to cooperate.

Preparing for the Arraignment

If your abuser was arrested, you may have already spoken with the prosecutor at the police station or on the phone, or even from the hospital if you are recovering from injuries. But a lengthy interview before the arraignment is important so that the prosecutor will have all the vital information needed to plan how to prosecute the offender and how best to protect you during this time.

While the police focused on the single crime against you that resulted in the arrest of your violent partner, the prosecutor will consider the big picture, looking for ways to make this case stronger, whether you go to trial or work out a settlement. Even if you never reported abuse in the past, talk about it now and tell what resulted from past incidents. Tell the prosecutor exactly what he did, name any witnesses, and whether you have any physical evidence. Be forthcoming, because this history is critical to show the continuing danger that exists.

If you filed past complaints that were not followed by an arrest, he can now be charged with these crimes and face compounded jail time. For example, he could be given five consecutive sentences, adding up to many more years in jail than he would have gotten for the current violent incident alone. By bringing in the uncharged crimes of the past, the prosecutor can show evidence of a history of abuse and make the jury care more about your safety. The jurors may not care very much about a slap in the face or a punch in the eye, but when considering a string of uncharged past crimes, they might be less lenient.

Evidence from the scene is critical to your case,

too. It corroborates your testimony. If you are hit with the base of a heavy lamp, the prosecutor can present this weapon in court, letting the jurors feel the weight and hold it in their hands. The judge and jury can be shown pictures taken over the period of healing of your injuries, or they can watch a video-tape taken in the hospital after you were beaten up. They can listen to the 911 tape and hear your fear and appreciate the danger of the situation. They can listen to his rage and threats on an answering machine.

Building a case involves a great deal of paperwork to be done before the arraignment, which can be as soon as twenty-four hours after the arrest. With your help, the prosecutor begins drafting the documents needed for the court. This includes your police reports, medical reports, the application for a protective order, and the bail application. Once the papers are filed with the court, the abuser, if he has not been arrested by police, can be arrested, fingerprinted, and brought in for arraignment. (Arraignments in some communities can be held late into the night.)

Applications for protective orders are discussed in the next chapter. The bail application is another critical document. This helps to determine how long your abusive partner will be confined in jail. Your prosecutor will discuss bail with you because he or she must submit a recommendation that bail be high enough to keep the abusive man in jail as long as possible.

The purpose of bail is to make sure the offender returns to appear in court. The prosecutor will request that bail be as high as possible to keep him from making bail. If he has a past history of domestic violence, or any other crime, it will be easier to get a high bail. Your abuser's attorney will be petitioning for low bail so his client can continue to go to work or go home. The judge will decide.

Bail applications are presented to a judge at arraignment. In a city with a large volume of cases to arraign, the bail application might be presented by someone from the prosecutor's office who is not well informed about the background of your case, but is scanning the paperwork in order to describe the reasons for asking a particular amount of bail. If your case is strong and well documented and you are obviously involved and interested, then just reading the report will set the tone. You or your attorney can press the point that you will be in greater danger if your abuser is let out of jail.

The bail system can create very real dangers for you because no matter how well the prosecutor pleads for high bail, there is no way to know what will happen. Also, the prosecutor may for some reason set the bail request too low. In 1996 a man with a history of abuse was released on $500 bail. When he violated the terms of bail, he was brought in again, and the prosecutor requested that bail be set at $1,500, which the man paid by producing a wad of bills from his pocket. While police and prosecutors argued over who was responsible for keeping the man in custody, the man walked out of court and later went to his wife's office and fatally shot her. Newspaper stories appear almost daily about dangerous men being free on bail.

Your abusive partner will be in jail until he can make bail or the case is dismissed. This often happens within a few hours and he will be free until his trial. When he is arrested, tell the prosecutor you want it to be a condition of bail that your partner cannot come to your home or workplace, harass you, or hurt you. In some cities prisons are now required to notify women when their abusive partners are released from jail. This time during the arraignment process while your abuser is in jail is a window of opportunity to plan for your safety. Get a protective order, and have your locks changed.

The Arraignment

Once the abusive man has been arrested, he will be held in custody until his arraignment, which is a hearing in criminal court before a judge that usually takes place within forty-eight hours of the arrest if the defendant is still in jail. In some cities courts are open until very late at night for arraignments. The arresting police officer and your prosecutor or domestic violence advocate will be there, too. Normally, you do not need to be present. This is when the abuser is told what he is charged with and the court decides what to do about it.

The arraignment is the time your abusive partner pleads guilty or not guilty to the charges against him. This is an emotional time, and there is pressure to resolve the issue immediately with a nonjail disposition. Judges are often anxious to do this, too. However, a conscientious prosecutor will not make any settlement deals at this point.

If your abuser pleads not guilty, the judge will set a date for a trial and decide on the amount of bail. A judge can also dismiss the charges if he or she believes there is not enough evidence to proceed. In rare cases the judge may deny bail and keep the abuser locked up. It can be several months before the trial, and there will probably be delays throughout the process.

If your abusive partner pleads guilty, there will not be a trial. Instead, the prosecutor and defense attorney work out a plan with you and your abusive partner for settlement. The judge will decide if he should pay a fine, go to jail, enter a treatment program, or be released on probation.

After the Arraignment

If the case is not dismissed, the prosecutor prepares for either a settlement or a trial. If your abusive partner is accused of a felony like stabbing you and causing serious injury, a grand jury will hear the case to decided on appropriate charges. Then the discovery process begins. This means your abusive partner and his attorney, who may be the public defender, have a right to know the evidence against the abuser. The defense attorney will also do some muckraking to try and ruin your credibility. Your life now becomes subject to review, so it is important to tell the prosecutor everything about your past that could possibly be used against you, such as problems with drugs or alcohol or infidelity. The prosecutor is your attorney and needs to be able to rebut any charges against you.

If your case is a misdemeanor such as simple assault, it is usually handled quickly, within ninety days. It could take six to eight months to get a felony case to trial. Your abusive partner's lawyer will try to stretch that out, so that the case gets weaker and weaker as it drags on. Memories fade, witnesses disappear, and evidence gets lost.

Acquittal with Conditions

In some communities if a man pleads guilty to domestic violence charges, the court will ask both attorneys to sit down with you and your abusive partner to work out a settlement. The terms are set with the court and are included in a protective order. If your abusive partner does not violate the plan in six months, the charges against him can be dismissed. If he does violate the settlement, then the case comes back to the court for further action. A significant number of domestic violence cases are resolved this way because many women just want a protective order and some kind of controls placed on the man so the violence will stop.

Under this type of settlement, in addition to an order to stay away from you, your abusive partner may have to provide financial support, enter a batterer's counseling program, or get rehabilitation for drugs or alcohol. If you agree to a settlement like this, make sure you have a safety plan to protect yourself, as outlined in chapter 7.

A Plea Bargain

A plea bargain is sometimes cynically considered a way for a criminal to get off on lesser charges, and this is true. But plea bargaining is also an efficient tool in the justice system. A plea bargain affords you and the prosecuting attorney a chance to consider the strength and weaknesses of your case—purely from a criminal justice and legal point of view. How strong is the case against the abuser? How much time will it take to go to trial? Is he likely to be convicted? A plea may be a more appropriate path if the prosecutor suspects the jury will not be sympathetic to your case or if the evidence is weak.

Plea bargains can assure convictions and sentences, speed up the court process, and prevent unnecessary trauma or inconvenience if you are nervous about testifying in a court trial. A plea bargain can lower an assault charge from a felony to a misdemeanor such as harassment, for example. But a felony could also be bargained down only one count, in which case he could still go to jail. The prosecutor should talk with you before any plea bargain is finalized in a felony case.

Sometimes a plea bargain is obtained before a trial even when your abuser claims he is not guilty. This is an agreement between the state and the defendant that in return for a guilty plea without a trial, the judge will consider the prosecutor's recommendation to impose a particular sentence. How severe do you believe the punishment should be? Does your abusive partner deserve jail time, probation, or batterer's education? Try to be as objective as you can, and express all of your concerns, fears, and feelings about your partner.

If There Is a Trial

If your case goes to trial, the prosecutor, acting on your behalf, will try to prove to a judge and/or jury that your abusive partner committed the crime. Your abusive partner will be represented by his own attorney and will have a chance to defend himself. You are the plaintiff, and he is the defendant.

States differ in handling misdemeanor and felony trials. In Nevada, for example, a trial for a misdemeanor will be in front of a judge but not a jury. This is sometimes called a bench trial. (There is some evidence that abusive men are acquitted more often in a bench trial.) The prosecutor may present the evidence, including your testimony or testimony of witnesses and police officers, as well as photos, medical records, and phyisical evidence. Your abusive partner, of course, has a right to present evidence to show that he is not guilty.

If You Testify

Once you agree to testify, your abusive partner may try to get you to change your testimony. Many women are threatened or coerced. Tell the police or prosecutor if this happens. Even if your abuser is in jail, he may send a friend or relative out in his behalf to harass you and intimidate you or beg you not to testify. If this happens, report it immediately. Tampering with a witness is a crime, and your abuser or his friend or relative should be arrested.

The prosecutor will discuss strategy and prepare you for taking the stand, telling you what questions he or she will ask. Here are some guidelines for testimony preparation gathered from domestic violence organizations, including the New Hampshire Attorney General's office of Victim and Witness Assistance, the legal office of the Pennsylvania Coalition Against Domestic Violence, and the Texas Council Against Family Violence:

- Talk with your prosecutor about rehearsing your testimony so you will remember all the details and the sequence of your story. Have a friend act as the prosecutor and the defense attorney and ask you questions. You are about to tell a story relating the details of what happened to you, so tell it as well as you can.

- Learn all addresses and dates and other information that you may be asked for. It is O.K. to keep notes in front of you. Bring all of your records and reports with you.

- If you have children, arrange to have a friend stay with them unless they are also scheduled to testify in court. Ask your relatives to stay away if their presence will inflame your abusive partner or make you apprehensive.

- Keep everyone concerned with your case—the domestic violence shelter, the advocate, or your employer, for example—informed about court dates.

- Arrive half an hour early so you can enter the courtroom, sit quietly, and concentrate on what you are about to do. Get used to the feel of the place.

- If you have a new boyfriend or husband, do not bring him to court, even if he wants to provide moral support for you.

When you do take the stand, consider these suggestions:

- Take your time and ask to have a question repeated or rephrased if you do not understand it.
- Give only facts, not opinions. If you do not know an answer, say so.
- Don't fidget or look down while you speak.
- Answer only the question that is asked of you. Do not volunteer additional information or make jokes. Nervousness often prompts people to keep talking or make wisecracks.
- Take a deep breath and speak slowly and clearly so that everyone on the jury can understand the significance of what you are saying, and the court reporter can take it down.
- If a question is about distance or time and your answer is only an estimate, be sure you say it is only an estimate.
- If the defense attorney raises an objection to something you say, stop your answer immediately and wait until the court gives a ruling. Also do this if the prosecutor objects to a question from the defense attorney.

- Do not respond angrily to anything your partner says on the stand. He may lie under oath.
- Do not respond angrily to your partner's attorney, who will try very hard to rattle you and show that you are not a reliable witness.
- Remain polite and firm. Pay attention to the questions, but do not let anyone put words in your mouth.
- Try not to look at your attorney or advocate each time you are asked a question. It can make it seem as if you need to be coached.
- During recesses avoid talking about the case in the hall or rest rooms.

If Your Children or Family Members Testify

There may be other people called on to testify as witnesses. You will know about this in advance if they are coming to testify for you or for your abuser. Witnesses for you may include the arresting police officer, doctors who treated you at the hospital, neighbors, relatives, and your children.

Most women want to spare their children the burden of testifying in court, but sometimes it can be a positive experience for them. If they have been witnessing violence in their homes for a long time and have feared for your safety and their own, it gives them a chance to say that what happened was wrong. However, it also puts your children at risk for retaliation from the abusive man, and they may be too afraid to testify. Discuss this strategy thoroughly with the prosecutor. It may be a good idea to coach the children, bring them into the courtroom when it is empty and let them become familiar with it. This can be done several times, until they feel comfortable.

People you know may also be called as witnesses for the defense. Even people in your family may agree with your abusive partner's philosophy and will say what a great guy he is, what a model citizen, loving father, good provider. And he may be all of these things, but he is also a controlling man who believes he has a right to use violence in his intimate relationship. Others may not be aware of this. Don't be surprised if people you thought were friends try to make you look bad by testifying for the defense. The prosecutor will know who the witnesses will be, and you will have a chance to discuss this ahead of time. Still, it may hurt and make you feel worse.

The Sentencing

If your abusive partner is found not guilty, he will go free immediately. If he is found guilty, the judge will consider your wishes at the time of sentencing, or you can submit a written statement that the prosecutor will read in court. A presentence investigation may be conducted, and you may wish to be involved in this process with the court's probation office. You can ask that the sentence include jail time, no contact with you or your children, a fine, restitution, payment of damages and medical bills, that he enter a batterer's program, or any combination of these. Make sure you understand the terms of the disposition because your abuser may lie to you. The probation department of the court supervises and oversees sentencing decreed by the court. Get the names and the phone numbers of the probation officer and parole officer assigned to the case. You can call them if you know your abuser is violating the terms of his sentence.

If he receives no sentence and is free—or will soon be free—it is important that you develop a safety plan for you and your family, making sure your protective order has all the terms you need. See the next chapter.

Jail Time

If your partner goes to jail, ask the court to notify you when he is released. Make this request in writing. This way, you can take special precautions to make sure you are safe upon his release. Ask the prosecutor to tell you when your partner is up for parole so you can come to the parole hearing and give your opinion on whether it should be granted.

Some cities, including New York, are establishing a special hot line with the Department of Corrections so that women will be notified when their abusive partner is released from custody.

Counseling as Punishment

There are counseling programs in many communities that try to teach men how to express anger without violence. It does help some men, but not all. Entry into these programs is often mandated by the court in domestic violence cases. However, if a man is offered a choice of ninety days in jail or mandatory attendance in a counseling program for batterers, he will choose the program. It is simply a way to avoid jail time.

It is generally agreed among domestic violence advocates and professionals that using attendance in a counseling program to divert the offender from prison is a dangerous practice that reinforces the belief that domestic violence is not a crime and gives the abuser a method of avoiding consequences for his violence.

However, some domestic violence law enforcement officers believe that rather than sending abusers to jails where they will be surrounded by hardened criminals, they should be sent to a program that teaches them alternative ways to express anger. There are many programs in the country, some of which get excellent results. But because there is no system for evaluating these programs, there is a move under way to require certification from batterer's programs before they can be used by the courts in sentencing.

One way to convince the judge that such programs should not be used as punishment is to get statistics about men who have been treated in batterers' programs. Inform the judge of the number who leave such programs only to batter again and again. And remind the judge also that at least half the men who abuse women eventually abuse their children.

Probation

Probation means the offender is free under certain terms and the supervision of the court probation office. If he receives a suspended jail sentence or must make payments toward a fine or support you and his children, the probation office keeps tabs on him. Many men ignore the terms of probation and disappear—or try to disappear. They fail to report to counseling or avoid support payments. Even in a system with a sophisticated domestic violence bureau for the prosecution, the follow-up is often shaky. There are rarely enough probation officers to track down the offenders.

In communities like Seattle, Washington, and Quincy, Massachusetts, which do not tolerate domestic violence, the probation office has a strong record of enforcement. In Quincy probation officers release photos to the newspaper of offenders who are not complying with their sentencing. Because the entire community is so compassionate toward women who have left violent men, the offenders are usually spotted by someone in town and promptly turned in. As one police officer commented, "In Quincy a man who beats women cannot get a date."

These communities are still the exception to the rule.

CHAPTER 4

How to Make a Protective Order Work for You

The first two men prosecuted for crossing state lines to violate a protective order received tough sentences. One is in prison for life, the other for twenty years.

A protective order is a meaningless piece of paper unless it is properly enforced and you have a plan to protect yourself and you let all appropriate agencies know of its existence. Whether or not your abusive partner has been arrested, the protective order—also called a restraining order or stay-away order—is an important step toward helping you free yourself of the violence. This legal document may also entitle you to additional protective services such as cell phones, alarms, relocation to a confidential address, and other safety measures mentioned in the previous chapter.

There is no guarantee that your abusive partner will obey the order. In fact, many women have been beaten or killed by their abuser while a protective order was in effect. However, federal law has put new muscle into punishment for violations of protective orders, and local governments are beginning to strengthen enforcement of protective orders. New Jersey, for example, has a strong protective order that can also include restraints on the abuser's friends and relatives. And it can order the abuser to leave the house, the car, the children, and money to you. If he violates this order, he spends a week in jail—on your word alone. However, in many states the laws on protective orders are not so strong, and police are not likely to be watching your house every hour of the day and night, so you must do everything within your power to see that the order is enforced.

What a Protective Order Does

A protective order can require your abusive partner to stay away from your home, job, and school, and forbid him from assaulting, threatening, harassing, or stalking you. The order may also include protection for other members of your family, including your children. The protective order will spell out exactly what is required of the abusive man, such as entering a counseling program, how and when he can visit your children, and whether or not the visits must be supervised by a third party. Sometimes you can get an order of protection even if the abuser still lives at home with you. Such an order could restrict him from drinking or using drugs in the home, for example.

If you live in a rural area, your rights are the same, but rural courts have even fewer resources to protect you. Domestic violence advocates and protection programs may not be readily available. While the protective order may order your abusive partner to stay away from you, he may be allowed to come to the farm or ranch to feed his cattle. If he disobeys the order and attacks or threatens you, nobody is around to protect you or see that he has violated the order.

The Emergency Order

There are two kinds of protective orders: temporary and extended. The temporary order is also called a temporary restraining order (TRO) or a seventy-two-hour stay-away order. These are usually available after a violent episode and with the help of the police. They are valid until an extended order can be granted. The extended order usually requires that you go to court to petition before a judge.

In some states it is now possible to get an emergency protective order at any time of the day or night if you are in immediate danger or if your partner was arrested or has committed specific acts of violence such as assaulting you, slashing your tires, or if he is stalking you. Police in some areas can phone or fax a judge or magistrate to authorize an emergency protective order even if the court is closed.

An emergency order can be obtained on your testimony, even when the abuser is not there to tell his side of the story. This short term order is called ex parte, which means it was granted without the presence of the abuser or without his knowledge. (Normally the order must be served on the abuser in order to be effective.) Sometimes it is valid until an extended protective order can be obtained. Everything included in the temporary order can later be included in the extended protective order.

Who Is Eligible?

A protective order can be issued against anybody who is a threat to your safety. In domestic cases it covers a variety of couples: married, divorced, living together, or dating. You do not need to be a United States citizen to get a protective order.

If you are under eighteen years of age and you need an order of protection against a man you have been dating, an adult family member can ask for an order in your name. You may also come under the jurisdiction of child welfare agencies in your state, and the violence against you could be considered child abuse if the abusive man you were dating is over eighteen.

If you have disabilities and cannot get to court,

another person can begin the process by filling out a family violence petition on your behalf in court.

Help from Attorneys and Advocates

If you are involved in a criminal case against your abusive partner, the prosecutor is your attorney and will help you get a protective order. The application would be part of the paperwork for the arraignment described in the previous chapter.

If you are on your own in civil court, ask the court clerk if there is a domestic violence or victim's advocate in the court, or call your local domestic violence advocates for advice. They will have a great deal of knowledge about the court and the protective order laws in your state. They can also refer you to legal help if you want it. In Rhode Island and some other states, full-time domestic violence or victim advocates are provided in all the courts.

Your abusive partner might hire an attorney to fight the protective order, especially if such an order would bar him from his home or his children. If you retain an attorney, be sure he or she is acquainted with current domestic violence laws and the attitudes of the court.

In New Hampshire free legal aid is available through the Dove Project, which provides free legal representation to women in court. In New Mexico the Domestic Violence Legal Helpline has a statewide

800 number staffed by volunteer lawyers who provide free legal information. Call any of the following groups for information and advice about a protective order:

- local women's shelter and center
- state domestic violence coalition
- state bar association committee on domestic violence
- police domestic violence officer

Criminal vs. Civil Court

Domestic violence can come under the jurisdiction of both criminal and civil courts, but where you get a protective order may depend on your domestic status. For example, in New York State you may go to family (civil) court, criminal court, or the supreme court if you are legally married to or divorced from the abuser or if you are not legally married but have children together. If you are not married and have no children together, then you must appeal to the criminal court for a protective order

It is generally easier to get a protective order in civil court because this court is concerned with stopping the violence in a relationship, so the punishment for violations is less severe. This court may also arrange for counseling and other services.

The protective order from criminal court may be issued at the time of an arraignment and will put restrictions on your partner's violent behavior, but it may be difficult to include child custody or support arrangements, which are usually the jurisdiction of family court. If your order is part of a police action or criminal charges against the abuser, you have the help of the district attorney, so the burden of prosecution is not on you. In criminal court you will need more evidence to prove your case.

If you live in an area with district courts or circuit courts, the jurisdictions may be different. Find out the procedures from your domestic violence advocates.

The Application Process

The normal procedure for obtaining a protective order is to fill out an application, get a hearing date from the court, and make your plea before a judge. Application forms for orders of protection are generally available from police departments, state's attorney's office, courthouses, and domestic violence advocates and shelters. The application will include your description of the domestic violence and a list of what you want the order to do. Small fees may be involved, but protective orders are generally free of charge if your application is accompanied by a police report. If you hire a lawyer to petition for you, then you will have legal fees to pay.

Be as precise as you can in describing what happened. Use exact dates and quotes if you remember them. If you don't remember exactly, do your best in summarizing what your abusive partner said and did. Describe your injuries and what kind of medical treatment was required. Also indicate whether your abusive partner ever used a weapon against you and whether you ever called the police for help. If your partner threatened to kill you or you fear that he might, be sure to say that. Also list the requests for financial support, and state that you want custody of the children. Take your time so you include all the details.

The protective order will include only what you ask for, so tell what you want it to do. If the abuser must move out of the house, it will include an eviction order. If he must stay beyond a certain distance from you, the restraining language should be precise. Include not only your residence but also your job and any other place where he might stalk or harass you. You can order the abuser not to go near your child's school.

Write on a yellow pad or scrap paper first. Make sure your description is concise and accurate. Some applications provide enough space and others do not, so you want to be sure everything that needs to be said can be included. You may be able to attach more sheets of paper to the application if you do not have enough room. Once the protective order is issued, it will require more trips to court to get revisions made. So don't leave anything out. Laws about protection orders are not the same in all states so ask your domestic violence advocates for help.

A Checklist for What You Might Include in Your Protective Order

- Keep him a certain distance away your home, school, and workplace.
- Forbid him to stalk you. This includes watching your house or workplace, following you on the street, and threatening you by phone or with letters.
- Forbid him to own or use firearms. Although federal law now forbids anyone under the jurisdiction of a domestic violence order of protection to purchase, receive, or possess firearms, it requires you to secure federal enforcement *unless* you include this provision in your local order of protection.
- Keep him away from anyone else you believe to be at risk from him, including neighbors, friends, relatives, coworkers, and children.
- Obtain temporary possession of the house, car, keys, health insurance card, checkbook, passport, immigration documents, birth certificates, or other things that you might need.

- Require him to get drug, alcohol, or batterer's counseling.
- Forbid him from taking, using, or destroying your property.
- Order him to pay you for damages, such as medical and dental costs, attorney and court fees, property damage, lost wages, and moving expenses.
- Obtain financial support.
- Insist on obtaining custody of the children, and require that any visitation granted to him be supervised.

Bring the Evidence

Bring all documents pertaining to the violence, such as police and medical reports, photographs of your injuries, damage to your home, and statements from witnesses. Also bring any documents pertaining to separation agreements and child custody. If you are asking for support or maintenance, bring proof of income (yours and his) and a budget of household expenses such as rent, food, utilities, health care, and child care costs.

You will need to give the court a list of all the addresses where your partner might be found, such as his job, homes of relatives and friends, or known hangouts. Give the court his auto registration and license plate number, credit card numbers, and any other information that will help locate him if he is evading being served with the order. Also provide a photo and a good physical description of your abuser so that he can be identified.

Petitioning the Court

The court clerk will take your completed application and attachments and give you a hearing date. A hearing will be usually scheduled within a few days of the filing of the petition. If there is a legitimate reason why you cannot attend this hearing, you will need to ask for a continuance so that your hearing can be rescheduled. Otherwise your petition will be dropped, and you will have to start all over again. Procedures vary, depending on your local laws and court systems.

You can go to the hearing alone, with the prosecutor (if it is a criminal case), or with an advocate or lawyer. If there are witnesses, they would appear at this time. As you appear before the judge to state your case, your abusive partner might be there, too, possibly with an attorney. Try not to let him intimidate you. This is a good reason to have the support of a domestic violence advocate.

Remember to bring all your evidence with you, and tell the judge about the abuse as calmly as possible. It is important, so take your time and consider what you will say. Think of it as an audition for a play; rehearse at home with a friend or with your domestic violence advocate or attorney. If you are asking for custody of your children as part of the order, ask your attorney or advocate if you should bring someone with you who can confirm that you are in charge of their care.

Sometimes an application for a protective order will be denied. Many judges refuse to evict a man from his home because they may not consider the violence serious enough or they are uninformed about the dangers of domestic violence. This might be more common for rural judges and clerks who are often uncomfortable when presented with information about domestic violence among people they see every day. Awareness of domestic violence issues might be lacking because there is less public pressure from the media and the local community.

According to the Rural Task Force of the National Coalition Against Domestic Violence, sympathetic rural courts are the exception to the rule. Many state and national domestic violence coalitions and the Department of Justice are working to fix these problems. The Rural Justice Center in Montpelier, Vermont, is developing a two-day domestic violence curriculum for rural judges and court clerks.

On the other hand, the domestic violence coalition in rural Wyoming reports that Fremont County has an excellent record in granting such orders because the judges are well informed and there is a heavy police presence in the county, including state police headquarters and an FBI branch office.

If the judge denies your application, you can appeal. This will mean filling out more forms, but do it before you leave the court, and submit them to the court clerk immediately. Depending on your local regulations, if you appeal within a certain number of days, the court will hear your case again. Consider getting legal help if you have to appeal.

If you think you will be in danger in the courtroom, ask a police or court officer to walk you out of the courthouse to your car or bus when the hearing is over.

Who Should Have Copies

Once the protective order is issued, the court clerk will give you a certified copy of the order: in some communities it will be mailed to you. (Always review the order before you leave the court and correct anything that is not accurate.) This is your official record, so make several copies of it and keep one with you at all times. Keep a copy at work, at your child's school or day-care center, or with a relative or friend whom you trust. If you are working with domestic violence advocates, give them a copy as well.

Some courts will send a copy of the protective order to the appropriate police agencies so that they can serve the order on the offender. Don't rely on this. Be sure that the police where you live and work are informed about the order: give a copy to police in neighborhoods where you work or live or go to school. Give a copy to your supervisor or the head of security at your job (see chapter 8 on how to be safe at work).

If you lose your certified copy or your abuser destroys it, you can get another one from the court, usually for a small fee.

How the Protective Order Is Served

Unlike an emergency protective order, a permanent order is normally not valid until it has been personally handed to the abuser. Many abusive men know that if they cannot be found, then the papers cannot be served and the order cannot be enforced. Some states now have laws making the order valid as long as the offender knew it was being issued, meaning as long as he was present when you talked about this to the police or in the court. In some states a protective order can be served to the offender in court after an arrest or handed to him at the arraignment by the judge.

In some areas you may be required to take the order to your local law enforcement office, where two officers—because of the potential for danger— will be assigned to deliver it to the abuser. If they do not find him, then two officers from the next shift will try. This may be attempted for a number of consecutive shifts. In a rural area it is often difficult to have two officers available at any one time, so serving the order could take a very long time.

Another problem could occur in a state where laws are different on an Indian reservation or a military base. If an abusive man lives on a reservation and the woman does not, it is possible the order can never be served. The only way it can become valid is if the woman calls police immediately if the abuser shows up and hands a copy of the certified order to police as soon as they arrive. Then police can serve him with the order and possibly arrest him for violating the order by having come to the woman's house.

You might consider supervising the delivery system yourself so that your safety will not be compromised. Call the police during each of these consecutive working shifts to let them know you are counting on them to deliver the order. Find out where they have gone to look for your partner, and suggest any other possible places he might be—hangouts, banks, shops, and so on. If a law enforcement official is unable to serve the order on your abuser, you have the option to hire a private process server to do this, but the cost might be prohibitive.

Once the order has been served, a copy should be sent within twenty-four hours to other law enforcement agencies you designate. Include police and courts in the district where you live, where he lives, where you both work.

Will He Be Evicted?

If your protective order includes an eviction order for the abusive partner, he must move out of the home you shared. If he was arrested and you changed the locks while he was in custody, he has essentially been evicted already. If he tries to get in, he can be arrested for violating the protective order. This is the ideal scenario, but does not work everywhere.

For example, if the lease is in his name and not yours, then the court might not be able to evict him. On the other hand, if you are married and you live in a community-property state, he can be evicted even if your name is not on the lease.

If he has not been removed from the home you shared, it might be difficult to get him out. Police can come home with you once you have the protective order barring him from the residence. This depends on the local laws. If he refuses to leave in Texas, for example, police might not be able to evict him forcibly, because the protective order does not give them the power to do that. But in a state with stronger laws, they may carry him out bodily if he refuses to leave.

While you are in court, be sure to ask how this is enforced. You might need advice from domestic violence advocates who can tell you how this works in your state.

Protection in Another State

The 1994 federal Violence Against Women Act finally made it possible for protective orders from any state to be recognized and enforced in any other state or Indian tribal reservation. This measure remedies one of the biggest weaknesses in protective order enforcement—a protective order from one state was useless in another. When a woman moved to another state to escape abuse and the violent man followed her, police in the new state were powerless to arrest him. Even if she went to visit a relative or friends or worked in another state, a violent man would use that opportunity to beat her up or kidnap her.

The federal law establishes the nationwide enforcement of protection orders from any court and provides tough penalties for crossing state lines to abuse a woman or violate a protective order. This is known as the "full faith and credit clause."

In 1995 the first man to be arrested under this new law was sentenced to life in prison for interstate domestic violence and kidnapping. He had gone to another state (West Virginia), taken his wife prisoner, and locked her in the trunk of his car. When an Ohio man's ex-wife and son moved to New Jersey to escape his abuse, he continued to make threatening phone calls and send threatening letters. These he mailed to his ex-wife's friend in New York, hoping she would deliver them. He was violating the order of protection in several states with the letters and phone calls across state lines. The woman went to a national women's organization and with their help exerted pressure on law enforcement agencies. When the abuser landed at a New York airport in order to stalk his wife in New Jersey, he was picked up by New York police. He was convicted and received twenty years in jail.

If You Move to Another State

The laws exist but are not yet uniformly applied. When you move, the first thing you should do is bring a copy of the protective order to the local police and let them know you are now living or working in their district. If there is a domestic violence officer, go talk with that officer. Find out if you need to get a protective order for your new location or have the previous one revised. Your protective order should be included in a statewide registry giving police and courts in your state immediate access to its terms. At least fifteen states and Puerto Rico have protective order registries in the law enforcement database systems. The FBI, in conjunction with the Violence Against Women Act, is creating a national database. Yet even in the age of cyberspace, many agencies rely on phone calls to the state capital or wherever such records are kept.

If your new address must be kept confidential so that your abuser does not find you, be sure to show a copy of the protective order to any agency or person you deal with—including landlord, utility companies, voter registration, motor vehicle bureau, your employer, and your children's school—so that your address is not released to anyone. This will take some time and legwork, but it will help you feel more secure.

Revising the Protective Order

There are valid reasons to modify an order of protection. For example, if the abuser has been living in the home, you may want an order that requires him to leave and stay away. If he moves out, you might need a child-support amendment. If you have a new job, add your workplace to the order. In most states you can go to the court and file a petition to change the order. Remember to ask domestic violence advocates to help you with this.

Never violate the terms of the protective order yourself by inviting your abusive partner over to the house or by going out with him. This could result in criminal charges against you. If you decide you no longer want the order, then you can appeal to the court. In most cases, a judge will determine if the changes should be made.

How to Enforce a Protective Order

You are the enforcer of the order of protection, with the help of police and the courts. If the police know you have a protective order and you call to report a violation, they can come and arrest your abusive partner. They might routinely keep an eye out for you when on patrol. In extreme cases, with criminal charges pending, police, with the help of prosecutors, might actually provide twenty-four-hour surveillance.

Call the police immediately if your abusive partner breaks any of the rules of the order, hurts you, or threatens you. Once you have an order of protection, in most areas police have to make an arrest. Show them the order when they arrive. If the violator is gone when they arrive, they will issue a warrant for his arrest.

Keep a diary or written record of any incidents— no matter how minor—violating the order, including threats or failing to comply with terms of support or visitation. If you see him stalking your home or job, take a picture of him if you can so you will be able to show this to the judge when you want to renew the protective order.

If a man does not take the order seriously, and tries to come into your home or stalk you at work, call the police immediately and go back to court to get a more restrictive order of protection, if necessary. If an abuser is caught violating an order of protection, he can be put in jail. In most areas a violation of a protective order is considered contempt of court. This is a crime, and punishment can include jail and substantial fines. There are much stronger penalties in some states now, especially for a repeat violation of a protective order, which might be an automatic felony. New, stronger laws in New Mexico allow police to arrest a violator if they have probable cause to believe he has violated the protective order. On the second occasion he will automatically spend three days in jail with no chance of parole or early release. In addition to charges of violating the protective order, he will be charged with all other possible crimes, such as breaking into your house or assaulting you. Ask the court probation officer or the police about the penalties in your state.

If police do not respond when you report a violation, write a letter reporting this lack of action to the chief of police in your city with a copy to the state domestic violence coalition and the Violence Against Women Office of the U.S. Department of Justice. Also file a criminal complaint about the violation so that the abuser can be arrested. Bring the evidence of the violation such as a letter, telephone message tape, diary, or a photo you took of your abusive partner standing across the street watching you (note the time and date). If police still do not arrest him, go back to court and file charges about the violation. The probation department of the court can put the violations on record and go after the abuser.

Stalking Is a Federal Crime

Stalking is not limited to serial killers and other sociopaths. It is extremely common compulsive behavior of men who are violent with their intimate partners. Women with protective orders are often stalked. Men who believe they have lost control over you will follow you for weeks, months, and sometimes for years. A wealthy industrialist stalked his ex-wife for years in the comfort of his chauffeur-driven limousine. Some men alternate the stalking with gifts or love letters in a manipulative attempt to get their way.

If your abusive partner stalks you, remember, it is part of a pattern of abuse that can escalate. It poses a very real danger to you. Don't for a minute think he is following you because he loves to look at you and pines to see you. The cycle of stalking might begin with telephone harassment or threatening letters. He may watch your house, follow you, vandalize your property, and establish a pattern of psychological terrorism against you. If he gets no satisfaction from this, he will get violent with you and your family, break into your home, destroy property, or kidnap you. Murder and suicide is the ultimate act of the stalker.

In 1996 stalking by domestic abusers finally became a federal crime, but only after years of pressure from the families of women who have been killed by such stalkers. All fifty states have strengthened antistalking laws. Once you have a protective order, you may be able to get a special alarm or cell phone from the police or courts to summon help immediately if you are being stalked.

If you live in Des Moines, Iowa, you can get a cell phone free if you do not live with the abuser, have a restraining order against him, and are willing to cooperate with the police in filing charges. The Domestic Abuse Cell Phone Program was started in 1995 by the police department, the county attorney's office, the family violence center, and a cellular phone company. The cell phones are programmed to alert police.

In New York City, with an order of protection you can give police the authority to break down your door to enter your home if they are alerted by your alarm or cell phone. The alarm is worn on a chain around your neck like a pendant and looks like a car-alarm device carried on a chain with car keys. When you push the alarm button, it alerts a security company, which in turn immediately alerts the police. It operates only within a hundred feet of the telephone, so if you leave the house, there is no protection. (More detailed information about alarms and cell phones can be found in chapter 7, which discusses planning for safety.)

Remember, save all of the evidence of stalking. If he threatens you on the phone, save the tape recording. Take photos if you see him hanging around your home, and save any threatening notes or letters he sends or leaves under your door. Even if the notes are not signed and he later denies having sent them, a police forensics laboratory could prove that he wrote them. When a person is agitated, more amino acids are released through his skin, and this evidence will show up if his fingerprints are on the letter. He cannot credibly deny having sent the letter even if it has no signature.

CHAPTER 5

How to Get Proper Medical Treatment

The Medical Advocacy Project, a collaboration between the Mercy Hospital of Pittsburgh and the Women's Center and Shelter, was cited as one of the ten model programs in the country with state-of-the-art health care for victims of domestic violence.

Domestic violence is not only coming out of society's closet, but at long last it has also been given official status as a public health hazard. From a medical perspective, domestic violence is an organized syndrome with symptoms similar to acute stress disorder and post-traumatic stress disorder.

A 1995 study by the Commonwealth Fund Commission on Women's Health established that a person's response to an acutely violent event is remarkably the same whether it's from war trauma, a concentration camp, or domestic assault.

All survivors of violent acts experience common reactions including paralyzing terror, loss of control, anxiety bordering on panic, and the sudden realization of their own vulnerability. Acute stress reactions cause amnesia, nightmares, insomnia, hypervigilance, poor concentration, and hypersensitivity to any sudden noise even remotely connected with violence, such as a door slamming.

Stress pumps up adrenaline and jump-starts our readiness for fight or flight. The system returns to normal after ordinary stress. However, long-term domestic violence is like being stuck in overdrive. You continue to feel the stress, remaining vulnerable to many long-term health problems, including chronic headaches, hypertension, malnutrition, gastrointestinal problems, migraine headaches, palpitations, dizziness, hearing or vision loss, miscarriage, and other hazards to pregnancy. The psychiatric effects include depression, low self-esteem, substance abuse, self-mutilation, denial, multiple-personality disorder, suicide attempts, and murder. The visible short-term by-products are the broken bones and contusions that bring you to the emergency room.

Domestic violence accounts for 35 percent of emergency-room visits by women, and it is the single highest cause of injury to women of all ages.

The New Rules in Health Care

When, in 1992, the American Medical Association declared domestic violence a public health hazard, it urged its members to recognize it and treat it, which many doctors had neglected to do before then. The Joint Commission on Accreditation of Healthcare Organizations, the national regulatory board for hospitals, instructed its members to improve care to those coming into hospitals with symptoms related to domestic violence—or lose their accreditation.

So here, too, the changes in regulations have forced the system to respond. How well a hospital responds will vary, so it may help you to know what the response should be. Doctors and nurses now routinely look for signs of domestic violence when a patient comes in. This is part of the initial screening in emergency rooms. The American Medical Association, which acknowledges that its members have failed to identify domestic violence in up to 98 percent of cases, has produced a manual to guide its members in dealing with the injuries and illnesses resulting from domestic violence.

Going to the Emergency Room

Even if you have no visible bruises or broken bones after a violent incident, you may be traumatized enough to be in shock and need medical attention. Have the police, a friend, or a neighbor take you to the nearest emergency room.

Accredited hospitals are required to train all emergency department personnel about domestic violence from the security guard to the receptionists to the nurses, doctors, technicians, and social workers. This multidisciplinary approach is the most effective way for the hospital to respond to domestic violence, so don't be surprised if everyone you encounter asks you the same questions about how you got your injuries. Be as candid as you can with them. They are part of the network of interventions designed to help you, and you might consider this a safe place from which to report the crime against you. The hospital cannot let you go home if they are alerted that you will not be safe.

Keep in mind that not all hospitals are equally responsive yet and that some may take longer to adopt new policies and train their staff. Throughout this book, the most desirable practices are described. They may or may not be in effect in your area.

IF HE COMES WITH YOU
If the guard at the hospital door sees you approaching with a man who seems to be controlling you, the guard will report this activity to the staff inside. If your abusive partner will not leave your side because he is so "concerned," this in itself will tip off the doctor. It is characteristic behavior among abusive men. If your story about what happened to you does not match the extent of your injuries, this is also a tip-off. If you find yourself saying that you fell down the stairs, knowing that your abusive partner intimidated

you into hiding the truth, try to find some way to let the physician know that it is not safe for you to talk unless the hospital can promise to protect you. A doctor should know this and request that your partner wait outside. If your partner objects or becomes abusive or belligerent, the doctor can ask hospital security to remove him from the area or call the police. Otherwise, he can probably be convinced to wait outside or in the waiting room, but security will keep an eye on him. The security staff may also be used to transport you to different areas of the hospital, such as the X-ray room. You are entitled to be safe in a hospital.

IF YOUR CHILDREN ARE WITH YOU

If your children are with you, they may also be traumatized or hurt, so ask the doctor if they should be examined as well. Your children might not want to leave your side to go outside or to the waiting room with your abuser. The hospital can call a friend or relative to come for the children, or they can assign a security guard or staff social worker to watch the children until they can be taken to a safe place. A social worker may be on staff at a hospital during the day and, in some cities, until late at night. In most cities a child welfare agency representative is on call around the clock. So if there are signs of abuse—emotional or physical—they will be called to come and see your children.

IF YOU ARE PREGNANT

Domestic violence frequently begins or escalates in pregnancy. Roughly half of all abused women are abused when they are pregnant. And 24 percent of the pregnant women seen in clinics and hospitals have been assaulted by a violent partner.

The physical effects of violence during pregnancy are especially profound. You are twice as likely to miscarry and four times more likely to have a low-birth-weight baby if you have been beaten while pregnant. According to a study by the March of Dimes, more babies are born with birth defects as a result of violence against the mothers than from a combination of all diseases and illnesses for which we now immunize pregnant women. You are at risk for a ruptured uterus, detached placenta, hemorrhage, miscarriage, and early labor. You baby could be malformed, permanently disabled, or killed before it is born.

If you had not thought of leaving the abusive relationship before, this may be the time to do it. Ask the hospital to help you so that you do not have to return to the abusive man.

SCREENING FOR SIGNS OF DOMESTIC VIOLENCE

If you came into a hospital with a heart attack, doctors would ask about your complete health history—for example, what your diet is like, whether or not you smoke, and so on. Now they do the same thing for domestic violence. If you were at the hospital before, the doctor might check previous records. If they suspect domestic violence, they should ask you questions like these:

- At any time has your partner hurt or frightened you?
- Are you now or have you ever been in a relationship where you were physically hurt, threatened, or made to feel afraid?
- Have you ever been hit, kicked, slapped, pushed, or shoved by your boyfriend, husband, partner, ex-partner?
- Have you ever been forced or pressured into having sex when you did not want to?

If you feel that the hospital staff will protect you from further violence, answer any questions as candidly as you can. An alert doctor or nurse will understand your reluctance to be forthcoming about domestic violence and may try to coax more information from you. Most women are relieved to finally talk about it. But you should not feel pressured or intimidated. If you are not ready to tell anyone, just say that.

No matter how you describe what happened to you, the physician will look for common domestic violence assault injuries such as contusions, abrasions, minor lacerations, sprains, or fractures. He or she will notice injuries to your head, neck, chest, breasts, and abdomen—the latter two especially if you are pregnant. Numerous injuries on many parts of your body are signs of either an auto accident, natural disaster, or a beating. The doctor will also look for defensive injuries like fractures or bruises on your forearm that would suggest you were trying to fend off blows to your face or chest.

In addition to physical injuries, the physician should look for depression, anxiety, and the psychological and emotional symptoms of stress disorders. Health-care professionals have been trained to ask delicate questions in a manner that will not embarrass or offend you. They have also been asked to refrain from using the word "battered."

POLICE INTERVENTION AT THE HOSPITAL

Doctors are usually required to report to police any gunshot or stab wounds or any other injuries they suspect are a result of felonious assault. If your injuries are less drastic, they still may report them in some states. Physicians in Tennessee, for example, although not required by law to report incidents of domestic violence, may do so voluntarily.

Doctors might ask if you want them to call the police to report the violence. If you agree to this, or if the hospital is required to call them because of the nature of your injuries, then a social worker or domestic violence advocate should also be present with you during this meeting. (See chapter 1, which discusses dealing with the police.)

CRISIS INTERVENTION

Some hospitals have a crisis-intervention team to help you cope with the violence you have just experienced. Immediate crisis intervention can help you work through the violent event and helps prevent post-traumatic stress disorders. It helps you ventilate your intense feelings in a safe environment with supportive listeners. The goal of crisis intervention is to help bring you back to a normal emotional and physical state.

To be effective, crisis intervention should include helping you plan for safety and to leave the violent relationship. It should also refer you to a women's shelter and link you up to the social service and legal systems, as well as advocates who can walk you through the systems so you can make progress. Without intervention and assistance from a support system, you are less likely to get help.

A few hospitals actually have a domestic violence advocate on staff. Mercy Hospital in Pittsburgh, for example, provides state-of-the-art care for women in abusive relationships. The hospital collaborates with the Women's Center and Shelter for the Medical Advocacy Project. By providing a full-time domestic violence advocate on site at Mercy Hospital, the Women's Center can provide speedier crisis intervention. The Medical Advocacy Project was developed as a pilot program that could be emulated by other hospitals and domestic violence programs in Pennsylvania. The project, initially funded for three years by the Pennsylvania Coalition Against Domestic Violence but extended to the end of the century, is conducting an extensive study to determine the national impact on health care response to domestic violence.

Hospitals in your state may also be part of long-range studies on the delivery of health care to women in violent relationships. The National Centers for Disease Control and Prevention has helped fund studies in several states, including Massachusetts, Rhode Island, and Michigan. Hospitals in California and Pennsylvania are involved in studies centered on emergency department response to domestic violence.

GETTING TREATMENT

Tell the doctor what happened as accurately as possible, and also describe any past history of violence and abuse. You might feel embarrassed, and the doctor may feel embarrassed for you, but you will be sorry later if you do not get your story on the record. If you are reluctant to speak to the medical authorities, take a friend who can do some of the talking for you and provide moral support.

You should be given a complete physical examination, which might include a neurological exam and X rays to look for old and new injuries. The injuries resulting from domestic violence are often severe. Of 218 women coming to one metropolitan emergency department with injuries, 28 percent required admission to the hospital, 13 percent required major medical treatment such as surgery, and 40 percent had been there before.

Your physician should tell you what the diagnosis is and exactly what kind of treatment you need. He or she should ask you if you will follow up with necessary care and see if you need help in doing so. If your physical injuries do not require an overnight stay in the hospital but you are afraid to go home, doctors may be able to keep you in the hospital for observation until they can get you to safety or you can arrange for a safe place to go. They can also take you out of the hospital under guard and into the protection of a shelter or the police.

If you need to be transported for treatment, the hospital must see that you get there safely, without being hurt again by the man who caused your injuries. The hospital is responsible for referring you to an appropriate health care facility and following through with your case until you have gotten the care you need.

It is important for you to receive treatment for symptoms of abuse, just as you would receive treatment for any health condition that could lead to disability and an early death. Talk with the doctors about how this can be accomplished whether you go home or not. You may not be ready to leave your abusive partner yet, but you must get medical care.

If medications such as painkillers are prescribed, ask about side effects. If the painkiller will make you drowsy, your abusive partner could take advantage of your lowered resistance to become violent again. Avoid tranquilizers or sleeping pills because you must be as alert as possible. You cannot be walking around in a fog when your life is in danger. Discuss alternatives with the doctor.

MEDICAL RECORDS AS EVIDENCE

Physicians must document your condition and treatment and report any suspicions about partner abuse or domestic violence syndrome. This careful documentation is important because you can use it in court if you are seeking an order of protection, a divorce, or child custody. In addition to your name and address and the time, date, and location of the injury, here is what your medical report should include:

- name and address of anyone who is with you
- medical history, including diseases, injuries, and pregnancies
- chief complaint and your description of the abusive event
- a detailed description of your injuries, with possible causes and explanations (the location

and nature of the injuries might also be illustrated on a body chart)

- the physician's opinion on whether the injuries were adequately explained by you (if not, documentation of how the injuries occurred)
- the physician's note that he or she did ask you about domestic violence and your response to the inquiry
- results of all pertinent laboratory and diagnostic procedures
- color photographs and imaging studies of your injuries (you may have to sign a consent for a physician to take a photograph of you showing your injuries)
- if the police were called, the name, badge number, and phone number of the investigating officer and any actions taken
- the name of the physicians and nurses who treated you

As recommended with the police reports, pay attention to the details of your medical report. Because several people might be making entries into your medical records, errors might occur. Ask to read the report before you leave, or have someone read it to you if you are unable to because of your injuries.

The records should be accurate; if they are used in court testimony, the medical records are usually presumed to be correct if there is a discrepancy between the records and your own testimony. Ask for copies of your medical records when you leave the hospital or doctor's office if you think you will need them right away to apply for a protective order or to file a criminal complaint with the police.

Physicians who treat women for injuries inflicted by their intimate partners are often called on to testify in court to tell what they saw, the extent of your injuries, and how they treated you. They might also become involved as expert witnesses, giving medical testimony about the nature of the injury or condition, as well as any reasons to suspect abuse.

PHOTOGRAPHING YOUR INJURIES

Most hospitals have special cameras for imaging injuries. The hospital will need your consent to photograph you. Photographs of injuries should be taken from different angles, full body and close up, with your face included in at least one picture. Two pictures should be taken of each trauma area and the photos labeled with your name, date, location of injury, name of photographer, and another witness. One set of pictures can be attached to your medical record, the other locked away and kept as evidence to be used by you, the police, or whoever has your authorization, such as your attorney. The photographs can be shown only during legal proceedings that you have initiated or with your written permission. If this set is to be mailed to you later, be sure it is to a safe address, where your abusive partner cannot get it.

The police and prosecutors may also want to photograph or videotape your injuries while you are in the hospital if criminal charges have been filed against your abusive partner.

SAVING THE PHYSICAL EVIDENCE

If your abusive partner broke a lamp over your head, you could have glass or wood fragments embedded in your skull. These should be saved after they are removed. If you came into the hospital with blood all over your clothing or with clothing that is torn because of obvious violence, the doctor should remove this clothing and lock it away in a sealed and labeled bag as evidence. This material can be locked up until it is needed by the police, the prosecutor, or your own lawyer. Evidence should be carefully preserved, labeled, and documented in order to be used in court.

PROTECTING YOUR CONFIDENTIALITY

The health care system generates lots of paperwork, much of which could be sent to your home after you leave a hospital or clinic. If you do not want items such as reports or bills sent to your home, do not give them your real address. Tell the doctors and staff that you may not be at that address because your partner might intercept the medical reports and destroy them.

He knows they are evidence. Have your reports sent to your job or to someone you trust.

If the hospital already has your address on file from previous visits or from your medical insurance card, ask them to change this in the computer and show a separate mailing address. Women have often refused to get proper medical treatment for conditions caused by abuse because they are insured on their abusive partner's insurance policy and fear that he will find out that they are getting medical treatment. If this applies to you, explain this to the physician.

When you arrive in an emergency room in any accredited hospital, whether public or private, you must receive medical care whether or not you have insurance. In Quincy, Massachusetts, women leaving abusive relationships are given free medical care. In some states the abuser is now responsible for paying for medical treatment resulting from that abuse.

DON'T LEAVE THE HOSPITAL WITHOUT A SAFETY PLAN

Nobody with a life-threatening injury or disease should be allowed to leave the hospital. This includes injury from domestic violence. Because of changing laws, in many states doctors, like law enforcement officers, face liability if they suspect domestic violence and do not ask you about it. If you are injured and are treated by a doctor who does not bother to ask if you were injured by an intimate partner, your denials and excuses notwithstanding, the doctor or the hospital can be held liable for any subsequent injuries that result from domestic violence.

Naturally, they cannot lock you in the hospital, but if they advise you not to leave and you insist on leaving anyway, you will probably have to sign a statement that you left "against medical advice."

An accredited medical facility should not let you go home without finding out if you have or need a safety plan, if you have someplace to go, and if you need a domestic violence advocate. They should not let you go until they assess the risk that you might commit suicide or be killed by the violent man after you leave the hospital. In order to assess the risk, they may ask you questions like these:

- Has he threatened to kill you?
- Do you believe he is capable of killing you?
- Has the violence increased in frequency or severity?
- Is there a gun in the home?
- Does he use drugs or get drunk?
- Does he try to control most of your daily activity?
- Has he abused you while you were pregnant?
- Is he jealous of you?
- Is he violent to your children or outside the home?
- Are you planning to leave him soon, and if so, are you planning to tell him?

This last scenario presents the highest risk for homicide. If they advise you not to leave with the man, they will have to find you some kind of shelter.

If you are a minor, a senior citizen, or are disabled, the hospital might be required to report your injuries to other agencies. If it is, the report is limited to the information about the violence. Your entire medical record is not sent to the agency.

If You Visit Your Family Physician or Clinic

Many women do not go to the emergency room or hospital when they are hurt but try to wait until their abusive partner is gone. Perhaps they wait until the next morning, when he goes to work. Others fear that if they use the same doctor who treats the abuser, the doctor will betray their confidence and the abuser will find out.

What if the doctor knows your family? If you don't feel you can share your story with the family doctor who also treats your abuser, then find another doctor. Try to find a doctor who respects women and will not treat you like a child, one who understands the problems of domestic violence. Ask your domestic violence advocate where you can find the kind of doctor you need. Call your local health network, women's organizations, or the local chapter of the American Medical Association.

In the frenetic atmosphere of most hospitals and

clinics, some doctors worry that getting into the emotional and psychosocial ramifications of domestic violence would take up too much time. Physicians are now being asked to recognize these barriers and overcome them. You need to get care for the short and long term. Tell them that you have come at great risk to your safety and that you are trying to get help without letting your abusive partner know about it.

Don't let yourself be pressured or judged. You will know when you are ready for intervention. And each time you visit a medical setting and seek help, you are one step closer to freedom.

CHAPTER 6

How to Find Emergency Shelter

Until the 1970s, there was only one known shelter for women. It was opened in 1875 in Belton, Texas, by women who had been beaten by their husbands. The house in Belton still stands, riddled with bullet holes from the time an irate husband and his vigilante friends tried to shoot the residents out of their refuge. The women shot back and the men left.

Women's shelters are an important part of the lifesaving response to domestic violence, and for many women in abusive relationships, going to a shelter is the first step to freedom. The organized effort to establish women's shelters started in the 1970s, when feminists began calling public attention to domestic violence and the need for a woman to feel safe enough to take the necessary steps to get away from the violence. The first shelters appeared in Pasadena, California, and St. Paul, Minnesota, which also established the first crisis hot line for women in violent relationships.

At first women helped one another individually,

but once they discovered their shared experiences, they began to unite in their struggle against society's indifference. First there were small, voluntary shelters operating on shoestring budgets; years of growth led to a network of shelters that provide not only a safe haven in an emergency, but also comprehensive assistance to women trying to escape from violence once and for all.

Today there are more than two thousand shelters and safe-house networks across the United States, and still there are not enough. As the Florida Coalition Against Domestic Violence points out, "Animal shelters outnumber domestic violence centers (in Florida) by approximately ten to one." In a small state like Vermont, there are only fifty-eight beds and cribs available at all of the shelters, and they are always occupied. The Michigan Coalition Against Domestic Violence reported that 2,205 women and their children were turned away from shelters in 1995 because of lack of bed space. Tennessee, with thirty-seven domestic violence shelters, provided services to forty-two thousand victims of domestic violence in 1995. One New York City hot line gets eighty calls *a day,* and because only half the women can be placed in women's shelters, others must be housed in the city's emergency shelters. According to the National Coalition Against Domestic Violence, for each woman accepted in a domestic violence shelter, two are turned away.

Shelter accommodations run the gamut from overcrowded dorm-style spaces to private rooms. They range from a solid and large building with a paid staff and multiple programs, to small homes and way stations with a single volunteer to guard the safety of the woman escaping violence. Some are a visible part of the community, but 90 percent of the shelters are at confidential locations, where women are protected through a secret network much like the witness protection program.

Even the local police don't know always where you will be located. For example, a victim services worker or domestic violence police officer can take you to a designated location where you will be met by someone from a shelter who will take you to a confidential location. The police will not be informed about the location. This can occur any time of the day or night. You might even be brought into another county or city to be sure you are far enough away from your abusive partner.

The Violence Against Women Act of 1994 provides some funding for shelters, but most are supported by funds and grants from charitable organizations such as United Way and the Salvation Army, local government, and businesses; they usually operate with the help of volunteers. Some domestic violence advocates are seeking laws to make the abusers pay the costs of shelters. For example, with the support of the Michigan Coalition Against Domestic Violence, that state passed a bill in 1996 allowing shelters to bill the abuser directly for services provided to the abused woman and children. The Michigan coalition sees this new law not necessarily as a way to fund shelters but as another way to hold abusers accountable for their crimes.

Generally, there are about three children for every woman living in domestic violence shelters. Some shelters will not take teenage boys because their presence would intimidate some women. A young mother who has just been beaten up might not feel comfortable with a male of sixteen nearby. But this policy varies, and if you are admitted to a shelter where your son cannot go, the shelter will help you make other arrangements for him.

He would, however, be able to participate in support groups and other services for children at the shelter. Many domestic violence shelters have extensive services for children, such as peer groups, counseling, and tutoring. In Quincy, Massachusetts, a teacher from the local public school comes to the Dove shelter to tutor the children. The Women's Shelter and Center in Pittsburgh has a mental health counseling program for children who are traumatized by the violence. Refer to chapter 9 for more information about how to help your children.

Safe Houses

Safe houses are private homes whose owners volunteer to house women and their children temporarily, usually for one to three nights. A safe house, with fewer residents, is naturally a calmer environment, where you are cared for like a guest. Women without children and older women sometimes prefer this option because it is less chaotic than a shelter.

In rural areas where there are no shelters, safe houses are more commonly used to protect women. In Montana, which is almost entirely rural, there are only twelve shelters in the state, but there is a large network of safe houses and a twenty-four-hour statewide crisis hot line. Domestic violence advocates there are mostly volunteers who must sponsor flea markets and garage sales to raise the money they need to help women in abusive relationships. There may be only one advocate covering as many as seven counties.

A safe house is sometimes an alternative while you consider what you want to do or until there is room at the shelter. You can stay while waiting for a plane or train ticket or for the court to open so you can get a protective order. Sometimes a safe house is used as transitional housing after a shelter stay until you can find a more permanent home of your own.

Shelters for Older Women

Many women without children or older women resist going to shelters because they often feel like outsiders, surrounded by mostly young women and many children. It can be more difficult for older women to give up a lifelong residence for a short stay at a shelter and then look for permanent new home. Some may fear ending up in a nursing home, with no money to begin a new life. The Dwelling Place in Washington, D.C., is an example of a comprehensive shelter for elderly people that frequently houses older women abused by spouses. It provides services to help locate housing, a job, and benefits. Florida, with a large aging population, has some domestic violence shelters designed to accommodate older women. Many other states, including Wisconsin, Kentucky, and Georgia, are developing more programs for older women.

If you live in Massachusetts, call the state domestic violence coalition and ask for their resource manual for older women, produced by that state's Older Women and Domestic Violence Prevention Project. It lists agencies in every county where you will find help. This was a two-year project funded by the United States Administration on Aging to enhance services to older women who are victims of partner abuse.

However, if you cannot find a place you like, go to your local shelter. It may help younger women to hear your story. Ask the shelter staff what other options you have. More services are becoming available to women sixty and older.

When There Is No Room at the Shelter

Because many shelters have long waiting lists, you may be unable to get in when you want to. Even if your police domestic violence officer calls every shelter in the state, they could come up without space. In some cities and states, the law requires that you be taken to a safe place if the shelter is full. In New York City, for example, if there is no room at a domestic violence shelter, women and children are taken to the Emergency Assistance Department until they can find shelter. People sometimes sleep on desks and benches there while waiting for accommodation. In rural areas you may be taken to a firehouse or church or even a jail cell to protect you from your abuser until shelter can be found.

If you live in Houston, Palm Beach, or Milwaukee, you might be offered temporary shelter in vacant hotel rooms. In cities where this program, known as Project Debby, is available, domestic violence shelters use this network as a backup while waiting for shelter space. This program is being developed in other cities, including New York, Los Angeles, Philadelphia, Boston, and Gainesville, Florida.

Project Debby was established by Naomi Berman-Potash, who got the idea when she read about the shortage of temporary housing for abused women and their children. Since she worked for a hotel, she thought it a good idea to match up women with empty hotel rooms.

Project Debby works on the same principle as a safe house. It gives you a chance to be safe until a restraining order comes through, friends and relatives can be notified, or plane tickets arranged. Your confidentiality is protected because you are registered under an alias, and only the hotel manager knows the circumstances of your visit. The hotels often supply meals as well as linen and towels.

Project Debby was cited by a woman's magazine as one of the twenty ideas that can make America great. It may be available by now in your city, so ask your domestic violence network.

What You Will Do at a Shelter

If you arrive with only the clothes on your back, the shelter staff will help you obtain food, clothing, and basic toiletries. They may accompany you to court, help you find a job, and see that you get medical care. Some have support groups for shelter residents and nonresidents, and child care and counseling programs for children. You will have a safe environment in which to reflect on your options and make your own decisions.

You will be introduced to others at the shelter and assigned to a room. You will have time to settle in and select any clothing or personal items you may need. In many shelters the housekeeping is shared by the residents, so you may be assigned a regular task for which you are responsible.

Shelters often maintain a curfew so that the building can be locked up at night with everybody safely inside. You won't be allowed to call your abusive partner, and the phone number of the shelter is not known to the general public.

Shelters can provide

- crisis counseling
- emergency cash, food, and clothing
- referrals to everything related to domestic violence
- support groups and counseling for you and your children
- job assistance
- assistance in court if your partner has been arrested or if you need a protective order

This is the time to recover from the immediate trauma and feel safe while you work out a plan, get an order of protection, and talk with a lawyer and the domestic violence advocates. People around you share what you have been through. There may be little privacy and the shelter may be noisy and crowded, but you will be safe and protected, part of a community of women with the same needs and goals. There will always be someone in the shelter to help you sort things out, to help assuage your hurt and loneliness.

Other women at the shelter will support you in your effort to change your life. They will understand the temptation to call or go back to your abusive partner. They will help strengthen your resolve not to go back to the violence, even if you love him—if that is what you want to do.

The goal of most shelters is to protect you and help you get safely free of the violence in your life. The staff tries to meet your physical, mental, and spiritual needs so your stay will be pleasant and productive. A social worker might help you develop a plan for reorganizing your life. You won't be told how to live, but you might be offered some very good suggestions and alternatives. The philosophy of most shelters is that women already possess the skills to put the pieces of their lives together. They just need some safety and support while they do it.

How to Get to a Shelter

If you are aided by police or a hospital after a violent incident, they can get you to a shelter. Victim services or social services agencies can also arrange help. And you can get a list of shelters in your area from your state domestic violence coalition. Some shelters may be listed in your local phone directory under "women's centers" or "human services."

Shelters, especially in rural areas, may have a network of volunteers who can pick up women and take them to the shelter. An advocate in a nearby town might be alerted by phone, and while you begin to walk up the road, they will come for you so that you do not have to remain in the violent home. Some women are picked up from hospitals or police stations. If the shelter location is confidential, you might be picked up by someone from the shelter. If it is not a confidential location, the police or a social service agency might take you there.

A few shelters are a visible part of the community, where women go to participate in support groups and other services. If such a shelter or women's center exists in your area, you can go knock on the door!

Staying in Your Own Home after He Leaves

There is a growing trend to get the abuser out of the house, not only for pragmatic reasons—there are not enough temporary beds for all the women who need them—but also for philosophical reasons. Why must women and children be forced out of their homes and into less desirable surroundings?

While nearly every state and the District of Columbia have laws allowing judges to evict the violent family members from the household, many fail to do so because of concerns over the man's civil rights (see chapter 4). Also, it may take time for you to get him to leave. In a time of crisis, it is safer to just get away. While in the safety of a shelter, however, you have time to go to court and obtain the legal means to regain possession of your home. Do this only with a safety plan to make sure you are secure. The next chapter will help you know what to do to be safe in your home.

Many women are taken in by their families or friends during a crisis. This may be a good solution, or it may pose additional risks to you and to the people you are staying with. Consider how they feel about domestic violence. Are they going to agree that it is a crime and help to protect you? Or will they pressure you to forgive your abuser and go home when things calm down? Will they invite him over to talk about it, hoping to reconcile you? If he comes to their home, they could be in danger of his violence, too. If you do stay with relatives or friends, call your local domestic violence shelter for advice on staying safe and making the transition to your own home. Find out what all of your options are. (There is more about dealing with family and friends in chapter 11.)

You Can Always Return to the Shelter

The length of stay at most shelters ranges from a day or two in a safe house to up to three months in a shelter, depending on the demand and availability of space. After ninety days, if you have not located a new place to live or you are unable to return home, the shelter may locate transitional housing until you can find a permanent place.

Many women use the shelter stay to get resources they need to move onto the road to freedom. They can remain connected with support groups and other programs to reinforce their commitment to end the violence in their lives. Others go back home to their abusive partner because they are not ready or they do not have the financial means to leave yet. However, many women who go back also maintain their ties to the shelter and attend support groups there.

Your community may have social service agencies to help you find affordable housing. However, depending upon your situation and where you live, this may be a difficult transition. About a third of the women who come to shelters are unable to find affordable housing and thus see no option other than returning to their abusers. (For more information on finding a home of your own, see chapter 11.)

Women also return to abusive partners because these men threaten to kill them and all their relatives if they do not come home. Some women return because they still love the man and hope they can work it out. And when violence occurs again, they return to the shelter. Each time a woman comes back to the shelter, she is welcomed and accepted. The shelter, as all the residents understand, is the first step toward freedom and independence. When she is back home, a woman may continue to come to support groups at the shelter. Many women return again and again, and each time they get a little stronger, until one day, they know they can make it on their own.

CHAPTER 7

How to Be Safe Where You Live

What will you do next time you hear that danger-ous edge in his voice? Or if he punches you or grabs you by the hair or slams you against the wall? Or when you hear him pounding on your door, threat-ening to break it down? Will you freeze in terror? Or will you remember that you can alert your neighbor with a code word so she will call for help; or that you can grab the extra keys and money you taped under the end table and get away; or, if he is breaking in, you can press the button on the alarm around your neck to summon the police?

One of the most important—and productive—things you can do is to develop a workable safety plan and rehearse it, just as you would a fire drill, so that you will not be paralyzed by your fear when you see an attack coming. You will know how to try to defend yourself and get help.

Ask for help on safety planning from your state or local domestic violence advocates. Some have booklets or wallet cards with ideas for keeping safe. Others may send you a free handbook and other materials with detailed information about safety measures and the domestic violence laws in your state. They can also refer you to shelters and other resources so you can learn about them before you actually need them.

Any inquiries you make to such advocates will be kept confidential. In fact, you need not give your name if you don't want to. Ask that information be sent to a trusted friend so that your abuser does not know about it. By talking to people who can help, you will be gathering information and learning what options you have, and you will also be forming a network that might be able to respond to you in an emergency.

You should think about safety wherever you are, so depending upon your particular situation, you will need more than one plan.

- If you live with him, you need an escape plan for dealing with a physical assault at home.
- If you do not live with him, you need a plan to keep him from stalking you or breaking into your house.
- If you work, you should have a plan to be safe on the job (the next chapter is devoted to safety in the workplace).
- If you have children, you should plan for their safety at home, at school, and at their father's home. (Chapter 9 is about helping your children be safe.)

Before you make your safety plan, and after you have reviewed materials from the coalitions and shelters, think about the past incidents of violence and look at the patterns. What triggered it? Who else was around? What part of the house were you in? What time of the day or night did it occur? According to a survey by the New Jersey Coalition for Battered Women, Sunday night is the most common time for domestic violence.

Escaping from the House

Here are some suggestions from domestic violence coalitions for planning what to do when you see violence coming:

1. Avoid being trapped in any part of the house without a window or another exit, or where potential weapons are stored, such as the kitchen, bathroom, or utility room. If you live in a rural area, avoid the barn or toolshed which may store machinery. Keep away from areas where there are rifles and shotguns, axes, chains, mauls, and tools. As soon as you sense that he is heading toward violence, try to lead him away from such areas.
2. Memorize important phone numbers such as hot lines for the domestic violence coalition, the police domestic violence officers, the elder abuse agency, or your local shelter. Teach your children to use the phone to call police, a neighbor, or others who can help. Do not put these numbers into

your telephone's memory for automatic dialing or your abusive partner could accidentally discover them.

3. Get to know the people at the local domestic violence program ahead of time in order to arrange for emergency shelter. Find out if they will be able to assist you in an emergency. Confide in a friend or relative you trust. It is important to develop a support network so you can get help. If you have been kept isolated by your abusive partner, this may be difficult for you, but try to make a start.

4. Plan escape routes from all doors and windows, including the basement and upper floors. What path you would take from the house and where can you go? If you live in an apartment building with access only through the front door or the fire escape, how would you get out? Decide what you would do if it is winter and you could not stop to get a coat. What would happen in the middle of the night when nothing nearby would be open, or your neighbors would be asleep? Do you have a rope ladder upstairs so you can climb out an upper story window?

5. Think up reasons to leave during the day or night, that won't fuel his rage. Perhaps you have to bring something you promised to a neighbor. Or you left your bag in the backyard or in the car. Once you are outside, keep going until you get to a phone.

Call police or someone you trust to come get you right away. You can dial 911 on most pay phones without money.

6. Decide where to go once you are outside. Determine where there are public places open 24 hours a day, such as police and fire stations, and hospitals. These are good places to go because you will be able to get immediate help and protection. Ask a nearby neighbor if you can come any time of day or night if there is trouble. (Bang on anybody's door. Most people will help you or at least call the police if they do not take you in.) If there is no place you can go other than a motel, then decide ahead of time which one it will be and how you will get there. Go there from your house a few times so in a time of stress, you will see it as a nonthreatening alternative to staying with a dangerous man.

7. Decide how to get there. Do buses and subways run all night in your neighborhood? (Keep money or tokens handy for the bus or subway or a cab.) Can you walk to where you plan to go before he catches up with you? If you have a car, make sure it is always in good operating condition. If you have a bike, keep it in good repair. How accessible are strollers and carriages for the children? Designate a driver, someone you can call in an emergency to come get you or meet you at a predetermined location near your home.

8. Invent a code word to signal a friend or neighbor of your need for help. Call across the courtyard, or pick up the telephone and say, "I'm all out of coffee," or, "I'm getting a violent headache," or "Do you still have that red scarf I lent you?" Let this person know that this means they should call 911. Ask them to call if they hear what sounds like an assault in progress, or if they hear you or your children screaming or crying, or if they hear violent sounds such as furniture breaking or glass breaking. Neighbors often call anyway, when they hear violence. It is especially important if you are disabled or housebound that there is someone who can get help for you.

9. Pack an escape bag with some money, a change of clothing, and important papers. Also stash away some coins for a pay phone, keys to the car and house, and enough money for a cab—preferably outside the house somewhere you can get to it quickly. In an emergency you may be forced to leave without your wallet or purse, where most people keep their money, credit cards, and keys. Perhaps you can leave this bag with a neighbor or in the trunk of a car. Consider keeping a getaway bag of money and important papers at work. Keep enough available to pay one or more nights' rent in a motel if that is where you would go.

10. In a rural area where there is no one around to help you, and police may be miles or even hours away, it is even more critical that you become connected with a domestic violence network and develop a safety plan *with them.* You may be able to arrange a way to call someone who will send help for you if police cannot respond quickly. This may be a buddy system, where you and another woman check up on each other periodically, develop code words to indicate when you are in danger, and find ways to provide transportation in an emergency. You could alert your buddy, leave your house, and begin walking up a designated road where you will soon be picked up by that person or someone from the network. Or, you may decide on a place to hide until help arrives.

If You Are Elderly or Housebound

If you are unable to run from the violence, think about someplace in your home where you will be more secure, perhaps a room where you can lock yourself in and telephone for help or call for help from a window.

Keep and build a network of friends. Establish a buddy system with a neighbor, friend, or relative who can check up on you every day, someone with whom you can share your fears and worries.

Call your local shelter or state coalition and ask for services available for older women or the disabled. Domestic violence advocates in some states, including Florida, Kentucky, Massachusetts, and Wisconsin, are making more available to older women. Seek out other groups for help such as the office of the aging in your community, the Older Women's League, or the Gray Panthers. (More agencies for older women are listed in appendix B.)

If You Have Children

Escaping with children is more complicated. If events happen so quickly that you cannot take them, return as soon as you can with a police officer and get your children. Not only could they be in danger of being abused themselves, but your abuser may also decide to hold them hostage. Women often will not run from the house—even at risk of death—because they fear for the children or they are afraid that they will not be allowed back in the house by their abusive partner.

Include your children in your escape plan and rehearse it with them (chapter 9 is devoted to planning ways to keep your children safe). Identify a safe place for them to hide, or instruct them to go out to a neighbor's place as soon as they hear the abuse starting. Reassure them that their job is to stay safe, not to protect you.

What to Take with You

If you have been driven from the house by violence, you will need access to emergency services quickly, so keep important documents—or photocopies of them—in a place where you can get to them immediately, or keep them in your escape bag. Violent men often destroy birth certificates, immunization records, and school records because they know that without these records your request for housing assistance or welfare could be delayed and that the children might not be able to register in new schools. You cannot buy anything without cash or credit cards. If he takes away credit cards, keep the numbers somewhere. It is always a good idea to have your own credit cards, checking account, or savings account if you can. If you save a few dollars a week, put it in your own name somewhere. Give the bank your work address or the address of someone you trust. Let a trusted friend keep photocopies of all important documents, or keep a set at your job or in a safe deposit box if you can afford one. Make sure the following items are in a secure place:

- orders of protection
- driver's license and auto registration
- birth certificates
- social security card or number (yours and his)
- health insurance cards

- passports and immigration papers
- children's school records
- medical prescriptions, medications, eyeglasses
- medical records, police records, and other evidence of violence.
- bank cards, credit cards, and checkbook
- your personal phone directory
- your most recent credit report

You may also want to pack away an extra set of clothes for you and your children, small toys that are important to them, family photographs, or small items of sentimental value.

How to Keep Him Out if He Does Not Live with You

If you move to a new home or remain in the one you shared with your partner, you may be stalked or assaulted by him even if you have an order of protection. Always assume he will try to see you or break in, even if you have been apart for months or even years. Unless he finds some other woman to abuse, he will probably stalk you. Take all the precautions already mentioned.

If you are in a new neighborhood, look for a neighbor to confide in. Someone should know when your situation requires them to call the police. You will feel more in control if you do this. Let your neighbor know that your abusive partner may be lurking around, and it could mean trouble. Explain the terms of the protective order if you have one, so they tell the police about it if they call for you in an emergency. Get to know your building superintendent or manager before you tell them about your situation, so you can feel confident they will not try to evict you because of this.

Join the crime prevention or block watch program in your community. This will give you access to information about how to be secure, and it means others will be watching out for you.

Give a copy of your protective order to the local police, your employer, and your child's school or day-care center. If you live in an apartment building, give a copy to your doorman or building manager.

Until your life stabilizes, consider asking a friend or relative to stay with you for a few days when you are alone. Even having friends over frequently for part of an evening for moral support will let your abusive partner know—if he regularly drives by your house—that you are not often home alone. (If he suspects you are being visited by another man, however, it will mean more danger.)

Making Your Home Burglar-Proof

Make a thorough survey of your home inside and out to look for all possible ways someone could break in, as well as ways that you can get out in an emergency.

Shrubbery should be cut or designed so it does not obstruct your view from the inside or outside. Keep a clear view of the area around your home. Secure the garage. Buy fire extinguishers, smoke detectors, and rope ladders to escape from second-floor windows. If you can afford it, install an electronic security system.

Doors should be locked whether you are home or not. Have dead bolts and pick-resistant locks installed by a licensed locksmith. If you have a protective order, you might be able to get new locks without charge from the police or the district attorney in some communities. A chain inside the door is helpful, but don't expect it to withstand any force if he tries to break in. Most of these chains are secured with a screw shorter than an eyelash. Door clubs and rods to brace the door shut are better. Hang bells on the doorknobs so you will hear the door open. Use polycarbonate glazing on glass or thin wood panels in or near the door to make panels stronger. Consider replacing glass or wood panels with steel. Sliding-glass patio doors are special security problems, so ask for advice on how to secure them. Always see who is at the door before you open it. Teach your children this, too.

Consider putting gates on windows on the first floor for extra protection. If you live in a city apartment building with a fire escape or balcony, you cannot block access legally because you may need to get out in case of fire. However, you can hang some chimes in front of the window so you will be aware of someone coming in. Make sure window locks are secure. Basement windows can be secured with grills or bars that have safety latches. Air conditioners should be secured to the window opening so they cannot be pulled in or out.

Outdoor lighting should illuminate the perimeter of your house, especially the areas around doors. Lights that are too bright, however, will make viewing difficult. Make sure the light fixture is installed out of reach in a weather-resistant housing. Use timers that turn lights on and off.

Seek advice about security from your local police department's crime prevention officer or community affairs officer. They may have recommendations about window locks, alarms, and other security devices. If you have a protective order, you might be able to get some direct services from the police, like help in changing locks or routine surveillance.

Keeping Your Address Confidential

If you do not want your abusive partner to know where you are, be especially careful about giving out your address. Addresses can be easily traced through personal records such as tax returns, medical reports, voter registration, schools, physicians' offices, public libraries, and video rental shops. Even the records for your eyeglasses can be traced. Think before you give out your real address to anyone.

Do not subscribe to any home delivery service—not the newspaper, the dairy, or diaper service. Avoid having anything delivered (most fast-food delivery is computerized so that your address and phone number are kept on file).

Use your work address or the address of someone you trust for everything. If you do not want your abusive partner to know where you are, talk with your friends and family about the importance of keeping your address confidential so that your violent partner does not find out where you live. He may try to charm or coerce someone close to you into revealing your address. He will say he just wants to see you for a minute or see his children. He will ingratiate himself with this person until they feel so sorry for him they relent. He may call one of your friends and threaten bodily harm if they do not give him the information he wants. He may pretend to be someone with an important message to deliver in order to get your phone number. Remind your friends how dangerous this man is and how easy it is to locate telephone numbers and find people. Tell them to call police and report threats or harassment to which he subjects them.

Precautions with the Telephone

Because your location and phone number are confidential, you might have to be the one to initiate contact with your abusive partner when you need to arrange supervised visitation with your children or when you have to ask him about child support payment or medical insurance premiums. Although you have not given him your telephone number, if he has caller ID on his own phone service, your name and phone number will show up on his display unless you have blocked the call in advance. All memory-based phone services, such as caller ID, call trace, call blocker, call return, and call cue (auto redial) might help him to locate you.

To protect yourself, you can press *67 (dial 1167) before you place a call, no matter where you are calling from. That way your name and number will not be given out. If you use a pay telephone, remember, the *67 does not work on pay phones, so if you call from a pay phone in your neighborhood, you may reveal your location. Better yet, get line blocking for your home phone. The phone company can adjust your phone line so that your phone number and name will never be given to someone who has caller ID. This way you can make calls without having to remember to press *67 (dial 1167) every time.

The House of Ruth Legal Clinic in Baltimore, Maryland, represented an entire class of women in abusive relationships before the Public Service Commission to obtain protection against caller ID. They claimed that the service substantially threatened these women and the people who help them.

Tracing His Harassing Calls

If he does have your phone number and calls and threatens you with harm, hang up. Then pick up the receiver right away and press *57 (dial 1157) and hang up again. Then call 911 for help, because he may know where you are. If the trace is successful, an automated voice will tell you what to do next. There is a small charge for tracing calls. Ask your telephone company for more information about these systems.

Set up your answering machine so you can tape a call whenever you answer the phone. Always keep the machine on so that any messages from him are recorded. Keep extra tapes available for your answering machine so that you can remove the tape containing the threat and take it to the police or prosecutor as evidence of his violations of a protective order.

Telephone harassment is hard to prove with phone records alone. The records show a call was made to or from a certain number, but there is no proof about who actually made the call. With the tape recording authorities can not only identify your abuser's voice, but also hear the rage or menace.

Emergency Alarms and Cell Phones

If you have an order of protection, police and the courts in some communities can help you get an alarm or cell phone that allows you to summon help in an emergency. Pendant alarms can be worn around your neck, allowing you to simply press a button to alert a security company, which in turn alerts the police. The one drawback is that the alarm will work only if you are less than a hundred feet from your phone. Cell phones, on the other hand, are portable and can be used anywhere that cell phones work. (Some do not work in tunnels or subways, for example.)

There are pilot programs in many communities with equipment often donated by security and telephone companies. Ask your domestic violence advocate or the police about these programs.

If you can afford a cell phone yourself, get one so that you can call for help wherever you are. (Chapter 3 contains information about these programs.)

Living Defensively

Learn to live as if you were in the most crime-ridden part of the world. Develop street smarts and always remain vigilant. Has that same car been parked up the block for a week? Is there an unusual hum on your phone? (Surveillance equipment is available to anyone in spy shops, and your phone can be tapped without actually installing a bug.) Follow these self-defense tips:

- Vary the times at which you do your shopping. Change your bank, supermarket, or shopping mall.
- When you go to church, school, or social functions, have a close family member or friend with you at all times.
- If he should follow you in your car, lean on the horn or activate the alarm to scare him away. Pull up to a convenience store or other crowded public place and call 911 or ask for help.
- Carry mace or pepper spray on your key chain. (Mace, however, is illegal in many areas, so check with the local police first.)
- Consider using a car phone if you can afford one.

This may sound like a paranoid way to live, but it is necessary until he understands he cannot control your life anymore.

CHAPTER 8

How to Be Safe Where You Work

Each employer shall furnish to each of its employees a place of employment free from recognized hazards that are causing or are likely to cause death or serious physical harm.

OSHA GENERAL DUTY CLAUSE

It is only natural for domestic violence to follow you to work, since most women work outside the home. And many men believe it perfectly within their scope of domestic control to confront their partners at work. He may call you repeatedly, send threatening letters, stalk you, or come inside and assault you. If he knows your coworkers, he may also try to charm them or harass them in an effort to reach you. He may ask them to talk to you or deliver his notes.

In 1996 a woman was shot in her office by her ex-husband despite a protective order barring him from coming near her. Police and prosecutors blamed each other about why the man was out on a very low bail when he had a history of abuse and had made threats to the woman. In addition, others in the woman's office were apparently unaware of the risks involved. Did her employer have a copy of the protective order? Did the security guard have a picture of the man? How did the abusive man get into the building without anyone questioning him?

In 1995 a woman who had a restraining order against her former boyfriend was murdered when that boyfriend showed up at her job. In 1994 a postal employee was stalked and murdered by her ex-boyfriend, a former postal employee who had been fired for an earlier confrontation with her. Three years earlier he had been charged with harassment for having threatened to kill her but was given a one-year suspended sentence and placed on probation.

Homicide is the leading cause of fatal injury to women in the workplace. According to the Bureau of Labor Statistics, 12 percent of workplace homicides of women are committed by current or former intimate partners. In any office with twenty women, two of them are probably being abused by their partners. A survey of women in domestic violence support groups in the Duluth Domestic Abuse Intervention Project in Minnesota revealed that 56 percent of them were harassed at work by their abusive partner. Women with violent men in their lives took more time off, were often late for work, or had to leave early; 24 percent lost their jobs because of it.

Employers Take a Role

While many employers still wear blinders and refuse to see domestic violence as a problem that affects us all, some are becoming more aware that violence in general—one in every six violent crimes—has entered the workplace and that domestic violence is a very big part of it. A 1994 survey of senior corporate executives found that more than half of them do believe that domestic violence is a major problem in society. A third thought it had a negative impact on profits, and four of every ten executives were personally aware of employees and others affected by domestic violence.

Business, labor unions, and trade associations formed the National Workplace Resource Center on Domestic Violence in 1995 to develop a model program of policies and benefits for employees who have been subjected to domestic abuse. The following year another group of corporations formed the Corporate Alliance to End Partner Violence. In October 1996 Domestic Violence Awareness Month was kicked off with Domestic Violence Workplace Education Day, sponsored by the National Workplace Resource Center with the governors of New York, Florida, and Washington addressing the issue publicly on October 1.

Local governments are taking steps, too. In 1996 the New Jersey State Legislature had three bills pending that address workplace violence. One requires employers of five or more people to evaluate all factors that might put employees at risk, such as working alone or late at night or in areas of unlimited public access. Another bill authorizes employers to seek restraining orders on behalf of employees who have been a victim of assault and other crimes.

Make a Risk Assessment with Your Employer

Many women are afraid they will lose their job if they reveal their domestic problems, but you are better off telling your employer the truth so he or she can help you remain safe at work and do your job with as little distraction and anxiety as possible. Talk with your supervisor, the personnel department, and security division. You are more likely to be fired if you don't tell them why you are absent, distraught, and so stressed out that you cannot function well. Just as the police, hospitals, and judicial system must intervene, now the workplace is beginning to realize their responsibility to protect you from domestic violence.

If you work for a company that has an Employee Assistance Program, they may already be aware of the kinds of programs that are available to you. In addition to helping you plan how to be safe on the job, they can refer you to shelter, counseling, legal assistance, and support groups.

Your employer may be able to offer you flexible work hours to handle legal matters, court appearances, or moving to a new home. Some companies may work out a way to give you emergency leave, especially if you need it for relatively short periods.

Sit down with your employer or union shop steward and assess the risks of the situation. Your employer needs to know what to expect, from harassing phone calls to armed assault. Once an employer announces a policy to protect employees from abusive partners who may follow them to the workplace, he or she will do all they can to prevent violence. But they need to know what they are up against, and they can only know that if you tell them about the potential danger. Some employers have actually relocated women to other branches of the company and given them new jobs to ensure their safety. Ask your employer if there is a trained crisis intervention counselor on the job or in the union who is trained to talk to distraught employees or enraged visitors.

The Polaroid Corporation, one of the first companies to provide help for employees in abusive relationships, suggests some topics your employer might discuss with you so that you can plan your safety:

- your travel route between home and work
- review parking arrangements

- safety of any child care arrangements
- status of current protective orders (give a copy to your employer)
- determine if substance abuse is involved
- security department and receptionists have a picture of the abuser
- an emergency contact person if you cannot be reached
- consider any health care problems
- job site safety
- special risks presented by your hours and work environment (for example, isolation or late-night hours)

Include Your Workplace in Your Protective Order

If you have a protective order, make sure it forbids the abusive man from entering or stalking your workplace, calling your there, or sending mail. Give a copy to the people at your job who should know about it. If you work in a large organization, that might include the head of security, your supervisor, and the human resources department. Give security several photographs of your abusive partner so that the guards and receptionists can be alerted to watch for him.

Be sure the police in the district where you work

have a copy. The police can also help you set up a crime prevention plan at work. Let police know that you and your employer will need their help if your partner shows up and becomes violent or threatens you. In most states, he can—or must—be arrested for stalking or abusing you at work, if you have a protective order.

Developing a Safety Plan

Develop a safety plan for work the same way you developed the one for your home. Think of all the ways in which your violent partner could reach you at work: by phone, waiting outside the building, or coming inside and confronting you. Figure out the time he would most likely come to your workplace. If he has a nine-to-five job, would he come on his lunch hour? If your hours differ from his, when will he most likely choose to harass you? Remember past incidents of violence, and try to see how these would translate to the workplace. Walk all around the site of your job, and trace the ways you come and go to work. Consider changing your route. Be aware of all the routes to exits in your building, which doors are locked or open, and where all the security cameras and alarms are.

Ask your employer about standard workplace safety procedures, and see how these can be adapted to suit your situation. Your employer might want to give you a panic button or beeper so that you can reach help as soon as you need it. Your personal protection can become part of the company's routine security services, including patrol of the building, parking lots, and garages; transportation service for those working late or arriving early; locks on restroom and stairwell doors; closed-circuit television; and silent alarms.

Some states, including Florida, mandate certain crime prevention measures for convenience stores, such as adequate exterior lighting, a security camera, and employee training. If you work in a public place such as a store, museum, train, bus, or airport, a cell phone or walkie-talkies might be helpful.

If you work in a private home as a health care or domestic worker, you should develop a plan similar to the one you have for your own home. Include this location in your protective order. Consider using an alarm pendant or cell phone, but be discreet—try to avoid upsetting the person you are working with, but remember that he or she has a right to know about potential dangers from your partner.

Here's a checklist of possible precautions to consider when making a safety plan:

- Consider relocating to another company site.
- Change your work phone number.
- Provide a panic button on your desk or work station to alert security.

- Obtain a cellular phone, walkie-talkie, or two-way radio if you work outside.
- Make sure your work area is well-lighted.
- Arrange furniture in your work area so that you are not trapped between an enraged man and the wall.
- Do not work with your back to an entry area.
- Remove clutter and obstructions from your view so that you can see anyone approaching.
- Keep the desktop clear of potential weapons such as scissors or letter openers.
- Ask your employer to consider using handheld metal detectors to screen visitors for guns.
- Make sure you are escorted when walking to the parking lot or bus stop.
- Post emergency phone numbers nearby.
- Control access to your work area via locked doors, buzzers, and card access.
- Sign up for special training offered to employees with high-risk jobs.
- Develop a buddy system.

If He Threatens You at Work

Your abusive partner might leave abusive notes under the car windshield. He could show up unannounced, or wait outside the building until you leave. Some men call ten times a day, ask for you, and then hang up when you pick up the line. It is estimated that 74 percent of women are harassed at work in person or over the phone. Your company should have a policy of removing anyone who appears threatening to any of the employees, so your intimate partner is no exception.

The chronic phone stalker needs to be confronted and threatened with legal action by an authority figure. If a coworker screens your calls, and still the telephone harassment continues, there are some immediate steps to take. Your employer can call the suspect right back and tell him to stop it. Or your employer can call the abusive man's employer, parents, friends, or other important people in his life and ask them to tell him to stop, or police will be called. Your company can also sue your abusive partner in small claims court, where he will have to explain why he made so many calls. He will have to prove that all of those calls while you were on your job did not cause you and your employer to lose time and money. It is unlikely he will be able to prove this.

Some Resources for the Workplace

The following organizations are committed to helping employees remain safe from domestic violence. You and your employer might be able to get helpful information from them about safety planning on the job.

THE NATIONAL WORKPLACE RESOURCE CENTER ON DOMESTIC VIOLENCE
A project of the Family Violence Prevention Fund
383 Rhode Island Street, Suite 304
San Francisco, California 94103–5133
Telephone: 415–252–8900, extension 25

Members include the following:
  Aetna, Inc.
  American Council of Life Insurance
  American Federation of State, County and
    Municipal Employees,
  Bank of America
  Bechtel
  The Body Shop
  Food Marketing Institute
  The Gap
  Kaiser Permanente
  Levi Strauss Foundation
  Liz Claiborne
  Marshalls
  Mintz
  Levin
  National Association of Manufacturers
  The Polaroid Corporation
  Reebok
  Service Employees International Union
  Wells Fargo Bank

CORPORATE ALLIANCE TO END PARTNER VIOLENCE
1457 West Alameda, No. 10
Tempe, Arizona 85282
Telephone: 602–517–0950

Members include the following:
American Express Company
Archer Daniels Midland Company
Bank One/Bloomington-Normal
Corning Incorporated
Eastman Kodak Company
Enterprise Rent-a-Car
Goddard*Claussen/First Tuesday
GTE Corporation
Hewlett-Packard Company
Lincoln Mutual Life Insurance Company
Master Software Corporation
Media Options
MicroAge, Inc.
National Football League
Park National Bank
Pennzoil Company
Philip Morris Companies, Inc.
PPG Industries, Inc.
Riesbeck Food Markets, Inc.
Southwest Airlines Company
State Farm Insurance Companies

Post office employees can use a toll-free hot line—800–EAP–4YOU (327–4968)—for access to a professional counselor twenty-four hours a day.

The AFL-CIO Community Services Program provides free and confidential services including help for domestic violence. Contact your local AFL-CIO state federation or central labor council for information or to find a community services representative near you.

AMERICAN FEDERATION OF STATE AND COUNTY
MUNICIPAL EMPLOYEES (AFSCME)
Women's Rights Department
1625 L Street, NW
Washington, DC 20036–5687
Telephone: 202–429–5090

CHAPTER 9

How to Keep Your Children Safe

I maintain that as the children of America watch family violence occur in their own homes, when they watch people who supposedly love each other be brutal to each other, they're going to accept it as a way of life, and I think that's one of the reasons that youth violence is probably the greatest crime problem in America today.

JANET RENO, U.S. ATTORNEY GENERAL

Six-year-old Ellen called 911 and cried into the phone, "Mommy and Daddy are having a fight. He's hurting Mommy. He's drunk." Then, while the police dispatcher tried to find out where she was calling from, the child heard a sudden escalation of the violence and screamed, "Stop it, stop it," to her father.

"He's near the new baby now," Ellen cried, turning back to the phone. "She's very delicate." The operator was able to get the address from Ellen and the names and ages of the other children. Then the operator told Ellen police were on their way and asked if Ellen could go to the door and unlock it so they could get in. But before the terrified child could answer, she screamed again.

"He's knocked out my sister." The dispatcher continued to give instructions and Ellen screamed.

"He's got the baby, and Mommy's got red marks on her neck." The operator tried to find out if it was blood. "How long has this been going on?" the dispatcher asked.

"Forever and ever," Ellen sobbed.

It is impossible to hear this tape without feeling Ellen's terror and pain. The police were able to get to Ellen's house, and although her father was arrested and taken into custody, he eventually returned home. His wife refused to leave him because she believed his threats that he would kill her if she did. When Ellen and her sisters grow up—if they grow up—they will have few recollections of their early childhood other than the constant fear.

Exposing children to violence of one parent against another is one of the most severe forms of psychological abuse, and an estimated 3 to 10 million children witness such violence each year. In most cases, when a woman is being beaten, her children are either in the same room or the next room. Indeed, some men make it a point to become abusive in front of the children. This is part of their power trip. One man menaced his wife with a knife while he held their terrified three-year-old daughter in his arms. One nine-year-old girl underwent years of therapy because her mother was killed in front of her while the girl was calling 911. The child blamed herself, believing that if she had called 911 sooner, her mother would not have died.

Children are injured when household items are thrown or weapons are used. Infants may be injured if they are in your arms when the enraged man strikes out. Young children usually sustain the most serious injuries, such as concussions and broken shoulders and ribs. The National Woman Abuse Prevention Project reports that children are present in 41 to 55 percent of homes where police intervene in domestic violence calls.

The Danger of Witnessing Domestic Violence

Even if your children do not see the attack, they will see the results. They see the bruises, torn clothing, broken glass, splintered furniture, and holes punched in walls. They see your face and the way you tense up or jump when the abuser enters the room or pulls into the driveway. Children are just as frightened hearing you scream as they are of seeing the abuse. They cower in corners, hide under beds or in closets, fearful that you and they will be killed. A woman who had been beaten often, and always late at night, thought her children were not aware. She carried on as normal a life as possible, never telling them about it, but saving money from her job to make an eventual escape to safety. When she told the children they were leaving and why, they never questioned her. Years later she realized that, of course, they knew about the violence. If they had not known, they would have protested leaving their father.

If you think your partner would never hurt the kids, think again. Even if he does not hit them or threaten them, they feel the fear. He may pump them for information, threaten to take them away from you, or turn them against you. They are walking a tightrope between wanting to please him and wanting to hang onto you because you are the safer parent for them. But they might feel they have to stay on the abuser's good side to stay safe. Children in violent homes are always in a state of hypervigilance.

Denial

When your children ask you how you got the bruises on your arms, or how you got the black eye, or why your face is swollen, tell them the truth in a way that they can understand. Tell them that your partner punched you because he lost his temper and that he does not know any other way to deal with his anger. Let your children know that violence is not acceptable, that it is not safe for you or them to be around this man, and that you are taking steps to protect all of you. Help them get rid of stereotypes about male and female roles in the family. Try to explain that the family is a partnership, with two equal people caring for children.

Growing up with denial of domestic violence distorts children's reality. If you and your relatives and friends all pretend that nothing terrible is happening, your children will learn to doubt their feelings and emotions, the palpable knot they feel in their stomachs that tells them that something is wrong. They learn that they must lie to teachers, relatives, and friends; deep shame keeps them isolated from their friends. They believe that no one else has this problem even though more children than they suspect are coping with the same kind of family.

Children often think the violence is their fault because they are often the focus of arguments that lead to rage. They see their mother accused of not being a good mother, of not keeping the kids quiet, of spending too much time with the children when the abuser wants attention. (This last is especially common among abusive men.) Assure your children that they are not at fault.

Be honest with your children about how hard it is for you to cope and how you feel so stressed that you do not always do the right thing for them. You are being called upon to provide more attention to your children at a time when you need some nurturing yourself. This is a reason why you should not be isolated. You need a close friend or relative to help you because then you will have more to give your children. Help your children learn how to do this, too, or help them find a special friend or relative with whom they can share some of their feelings.

Abusive men often prevent their partners and children from having contact with other people, even close relatives. This lack of interaction with others makes it difficult for children from violent homes to get along with peers and adults. But try to encourage your children to develop close relationships with a family member they particularly like, or a teacher who takes an interest in them. If they know there are people around with whom they can talk and feel consoled, it will help them cope.

Once into their teens, children escape into alcohol, drugs, sex, and food to numb their feelings. More than 80 percent of runaway teens are from violent homes. Their feelings of powerlessness may be expressed as anger toward you for not being able to protect them. Their beliefs will be influenced by our culture's tendency to blame the victim. And they may start acting violently toward you and others. An older child may become abusive toward a younger and smaller sibling. They see that the abuser gets what he wants with violence, so they learn that.

Children Taking on Adult Roles

Your children love you and hate to see you hurting. They want to comfort and protect you. Your ten-year-old son might try to be the man in the family, believing it is his responsibility to protect you from violence. Don't let him. While a boy might put himself in the middle of a fight and try to act like a man, he is a terrified boy who needs you to comfort him. If your child tries to referee, he or she can be hurt in the assault: 62 percent of sons over the age of fourteen who try to protect their mothers from attack are injured in the process; of the boys between the ages of eleven and twenty who commit murder, 63 percent kill the man who is abusing their mother.

In many violent homes young children start paying the bills or dealing with the landlord. They call in sick for the adult at work. They keep the household running by cooking and doing the laundry and grocery shopping. Older kids become parents to the younger ones. Household chores and responsibilities are good for children, but if they feel they are responsible for running the household because you and your abusive partner cannot, then it has damaging effects.

Until you are able to move away from the violent man, explain to your children the need to develop a safety plan for both you and them. Let them know you are trying to make order out of chaos and take steps toward change. If you remain a strong parent, and a consistent parent, in the face of the adversity, it will help your children. And if your children see that you are looking to others for help—advocates, police, friends—they will learn that there are other people who care.

Some children are affected more than others. Some bounce back once they leave the violent environment; others do not. The children who seem to do well in the face of adversity may have a better relationship with you and a good social support network outside the family. Some children are simply more resilient than others. Researchers have found that children benefit when they are geographically separated from the abuser.

Help from Your Children's Doctors

The stress of living in a violent home results in very real physical and emotional conditions. Your children can develop stress-related ailments like headaches, ulcers, and rashes. Anxiety and fear can disrupt their eating and sleeping patterns and cause regressive behavior such as thumb-sucking, nail-biting, and bed-wetting. A violent environment can take a toll on babies and toddlers, leading to frequent colds, and gastrointestinal problems. They may be slow to develop language skills because they are afraid to speak for fear of being the target of anger.

Doctors might notice signs of stress in your children during routine checkups. If you trust your doctor not to reveal any confidences to your partner, encourage your children to open up to the doctor and talk about their feelings. If you do not trust your doctor, call your domestic violence advocate or the local chapter of the American Medical Association for referrals to doctors who have experience with children who have been affected by domestic violence.

In Boston, Massachusetts, a program called AWAKE (Advocacy for Women and Kids in Emergencies) was established at Children's Hospital in 1986. This was the first program in a pediatric setting designed to support and counsel women while working with their children. Advocates, hospital staff, and outside agencies collaborate to provide safety for both mothers and their children.

Help from Domestic Violence Advocates

A call to your state domestic violence coalition or your community's child welfare agency can connect you with programs that can help you and your children. Many of the domestic violence shelters can provide or refer you to support groups or individual guidance for children's emotional needs. Such measures can help children learn to cope with their feelings in a nonthreatening environment, thereby reducing some of the harmful effects of domestic violence.

If you go to a women's shelter with your children, they will likely benefit from the safe, secure, supportive, and nonviolent atmosphere. Some shelters provide support groups for older children so they can talk out their feelings and frustrations. Children will often tell a stranger things they will not want to share with you because they don't want to hurt your feelings or incur your displeasure.

The Pro Bono Children's Mental Health Project at the Pittsburgh Women's Center and Shelter is the first of its kind for children of violent families, serving children of shelter residents and nonresidents. One little boy was painfully withdrawn in school. He was daydreaming in class and would not raise a hand or complete an assignment. After the child had five sessions with one of the project's professional volunteers, his schoolteacher called his mother to report a "drastic change."

The goal of counseling is to help children understand that they are not responsible for the domestic violence and chaos at home, that they cannot change it or control it. Counseling can help them identify their feelings, express them in a healthy way, and develop coping mechanisms such as talking it out, going out for a run, or even punching a pillow.

Coping with Problems at School

Children with academic problems might be worrying constantly about what happened at home last night or what will happen when they get home today. Problems at school can lead to poor scholarship, fighting with classmates, or withdrawal from social interaction. They may not learn how to interact with others because they never see it done in a positive way at home. Instead, they learn to be aggressive and act out, imitating the violent behavior they see. They cannot do homework because there is no place at home to concentrate.

Consider talking with your child's teacher about the violence; the teacher might well have noticed the signs already. Teachers are not permitted to question children about violence or abuse, but most are required to report child abuse—physical or emotional—if they suspect it. The teacher reports it to the school's principal, dean, or guidance counselors, who then report it to the state child welfare agency.

Children might not express their feelings but often show a change in personality. For example, a good child will one day explode or have a temper tantrum. They might put up a red flag until the teacher asks what is the matter. Your child might want to protect you, so he or she might disguise fear in the form of a hypothetical question to the teacher. "Do you think it's all right for a man to punch out his wife because she forgot to pick up his dry cleaning?"

In some school systems teachers are being trained to recognize signs of domestic violence and to teach children about it. Junior and senior high schools in many communities already have curriculums that include information about how to recognize and counteract abusive behavior in families and in dating. Some school curriculums are gradually introducing lessons about family violence on the elementary level as well.

Safety at School

If your protective order forbids the abusive man from coming to the school or lurking nearby to lure your child away, talk with the principal or appropriate administrator about this risk. Give him or her a copy of the protective order and a photo of your abusive partner. Make sure the school understands the order so that if the abuser shows up at school, he will not be allowed to take your child. Do the same if your children are in day care or a nursery school. Notify police in the school district, too.

If your protective order or custody agreement specifies that enrollment in a particular school district should remain confidential, then you must make sure that school officials know this. Ask them not to give out your name or address to anyone and to deny that your child is in the school if they get queries over the telephone. Women have kept their children out of school for security reasons. In cases where school records are not protected by law, violent fathers use them to track down mothers or kidnap children.

Talk candidly with your children about the terms of the protective order at school. Let them know what to do if they are approached by their father. Explain that there are special rules that specify how, when, and if they can visit their father.

Teaching Safety

Talking about fear is not enough unless children can be taught how to manage fear or anger and protect themselves. Children need to feel empowered, to know they have ways to make themselves safe, and that they can act independently if they need to. For this reason it is a good idea to help them develop their own safety plan. Even though you and your children might love the abusive man, you know that the abuse will probably happen again. By making a plan, you are letting your children know that you are striving to improve their lives and protect them. When your children can participate in the planning, they know that you are a team and that you will stick together.

If you have several children, you need a group plan as well as an individual plan for each child. If your children resist such planning, don't force them to comply, or it could make their anxiety worse. The safety plan should be realistic, appropriate for your child's age, and voluntary. And keep it simple. Include only as much as your child can cope with because in a panic, he or she might forget what to do if overburdened with details.

Ask them to describe the last violent episode from their point of view. How did they feel last time? What did they do? Did they try to protect you? Did they run away? Did they call the police or hide in the closet? Discuss all these reactions with them. This will help them think of how to be safe. Your children should suggest ideas for the plan themselves.

Use the escape plan suggestions in chapter 7 as a guide for the children's plan, which could include finding a way out of the house or calling the police or the person designated to help. Younger children might need to know where to hide or which neighbor they can call or take refuge with.

Let the children know that the very act of making a safety plan might enrage the abuser if he finds out. Assure them that if the plan fails, they must never believe it is their fault. They should understand that violence is solely the responsibility of the abuser. Assure them that if things happen so fast that you must leave without them, you will come back for them. Children also need to know the plan can be revised if necessary. Rehearse the plan with your children, but try not to make it seem like an emergency each time you practice. Try to develop it more like a routine, like a fire drill at school; make them familiar with where the exits are and how to leave the building safely. Children learn better when they are less anxious; excessive rehearsal could generate anxiety.

What About the Baby?

If you have an infant, and you have enough warning that the abuse is starting, tell the abusive man that you hear the baby crying; take the baby out of the crib and go out a back door or window before your partner realizes what's happening. Keep going until you are in a safe place. If you do not have enough time, don't pick up the baby, even if it is screaming or crying—the baby could be hurt more easily if it is in your arms.

Safety When You Are Not There

Before you hire a baby-sitter to stay with your children while you are at work or when you go out, explain any conditions about protective orders, custody, and visitation restrictions. Discuss and rehearse your safety plans, including how to handle your children's possible reactions. Explain that the father is not allowed to visit without permission, so that if he should show up or call and ask to meet them, the sitter will know what to do to prevent an abduction. Don't leave your children with anyone unless you feel confident that he or she will know what to do and how to protect your children.

Safety When They Are with the Abusive Man

You are at risk when your abuser no longer lives with you but comes to see his children. In the next chapter you will find information on how to set up child custody and visitation in the safest possible way. Many advocates and domestic violence experts believe that violent men should never be allowed to visit the children or that the visits should take place only in a supervised setting. If these options are unavailable to you, be prepared and plan for any eventuality.

The attorney Barbara Hart, legal director of the Pennsylvania Coalition Against Domestic Violence, has lectured and written widely on children and domestic violence. Some of these suggestions are adapted from her article "Safety Planning for Children: Strategizing for Unsupervised Visits with Batterers."

1. Children should know how to reach you by phone at all times: at home, at work, or wherever else you may be. This includes learning how to call long distance, make a credit card call, and get operator assistance. If you have an answering machine, leave it on at all times so children can leave you a message. Have them practice calling you and talking to the machine so they know how to wait for the beep and how long they can speak.

2. Teach them to call 911 to ask for help from the police or emergency medical team. Teach them to give their address and to explain the situation in language that will convince the police that they are truly in an emergency: "My father is drunk and

wants me to get in the car with him," or "My father locked me in and won't let me go home, and the court paper says he can't do that."

3. Keep a copy of the protective order with them. Explain your protective order to your children. Show them the paper if they are old enough. Even if they cannot read, they can learn to recognize it as an official document from the court. It has rules concerning how the father must behave during a visit. Let them have a copy of it to keep in their pocket or with their belongings. Explain the rules of the order and the consequences if these rules are violated. Make sure police in the father's neighborhood have a copy of the protective order.

4. Identify the location of all telephones as well as all possible escape routes from the father's house, including doors and windows. If your child is old enough, you may want to give him or her a cordless phone to carry. Walk or drive your child through the neighborhood in order to identify pay phones, fire alarms, stores, or other places they could possibly go to find help.

5. Teach them how to respond to their father when he tries to lure them away from you or to extract information about you from them. Discuss this with your children ahead of time, and give them a chance to think about it. Let them know that they must be safe first. This might even mean answer-

ing their father's questions. But it also means that once they come home, they can be honest with you about what happened.

Protecting Them from Abduction or Kidnapping

Each year in the United States, more than 350,000 children are abducted by parents. That's about forty kids every hour. Most are abducted by fathers or people acting on the father's behalf, including stepmothers and relatives. A 1990 study estimated that half of these abductions occur in the context of domestic violence, and many happen after the parents have been separated or divorced for more than two years.

If you think abduction is a possibility, then a safety plan for your children takes on another dimension. You need to talk about the possibility with them and teach them additional safety precautions. Here's a list of useful points:

- Teach your children how to identify location and surroundings: names of towns, restaurants, roads, schools.
- If they are old enough, teach your children how to read a map so they can help others find them.
- Teach them how to ask for help from people dressed in police or military uniforms, and how to

give their names, home address, and phone number.

- Teach them to leave notes on napkins or paper towels in rest rooms not likely to be used by the father. Think of other ways your child could get a message out that he or she is being kidnapped without disclosing these efforts to the abusive man.

If He Takes Them Hostage

If your child is taken hostage, he or she might face an anguishing decision: whether to placate the father or try to get away. Help your children understand how this situation might arise and that their own safety should come first. Sometimes a man will threaten to kill the child if he or she reveals their whereabouts.

Many fathers who snatch their children tell them their mother is dead or doesn't want them anymore, so talk with your children so they know that is not true. Tell them that they should not believe that you are dead unless they hear it from someone you both trust. Let them know that you will search diligently if they are abducted and that you will ask police to consider their safety before anything else.

Such precautions might seem melodramatic, but given the stakes and the risks, it is wiser to err on the side of caution.

Some Resources for Your Children

Many of the state coalitions, local domestic violence centers, and your public library have helpful information for children, including books and videos. Here are some examples:

It's Not OK: Let's Talk About Domestic Violence is an eight-minute video produced by American Bar Association president Roberta Cooper Ramo in partnership with the Walt Disney Company. Ben Savage of ABC's *Boy Meets World* narrates the video, which explain to kids why domestic violence is not their fault and that there are people who can help them.

When Mommy Got Hurt, a book written by Ilene Lee and Kathy Sylwester and illustrated by Carol Deach, is a simple, touching storybook for young children that answers many of the questions they have about domestic violence. There are black-and-white illustrations that children can color if they like. The book, which is often used by shelters in conjunction with counseling, can be ordered for $4.95 from Kidsrights, 10100 Park Cedar Drive, Charlotte, NC 28210. Or call 800–892-KIDS (5437).

CHAPTER 10

How to Leave Safely

For years, no-fault divorce and joint custody prohibited us from using evidence of domestic violence in divorce and custody. That is changing now.

When you are ready to leave for good, two things should be foremost in your mind. First, you will be at increased risk of retaliation now, so safety planning and caution are critical. Never leave an abusive relationship without being sure that you have enough protection and help from others. Second, the laws are changing so fast that it is imperative that you get legal help from people who are knowledgeable about the current status of using evidence of domestic violence in divorce and child custody proceedings.

When no-fault divorce became the norm in many states, some family lawyers stopped asking about intimate violence and eliminated marital misconduct from claims. Now they often fail to introduce and document relevant evidence for trial, and some ignore protective orders, police reports, medical records, 911 tapes, voice mail tapes, letters written by the abuser, and journals kept by women and children. Some fail to call in experts such as doctors and domestic violence advocates in cases that require knowledgeable testimony. In other words, they do not always pay attention to the evidence, much of which is crucial.

The good news is that awareness is growing, however slowly, among attorneys, who are at increasing risk of malpractice suits resulting from failure to address issues of domestic violence in custody and divorce representation.

Finding Legal Help

You may have instituted a safety plan, obtained a protective order to help keep him away from you, or lodged possible criminal charges, but to begin a legal separation and divorce you also need a lawyer. And you especially need legal help to get custody of your children, whether you are married to the abusive man or not.

Many lawyers acknowledge that their profession is remarkably uninformed about domestic violence, so you may not get the best representation unless you shop around. Choose only a domestic relations lawyer experienced in domestic violence and familiar with the latest changes in the law. For referrals call domestic violence advocates or your county or state bar association.

Legal services attorneys are often better informed about domestic violence laws. For example, 95 percent of the divorce cases handled by Legal Services in Oklahoma are said to involve domestic violence, so those lawyers are very well versed in this area of the law. Despite cutbacks in federal funding of the Legal Services Corporation, you may still be able to find free legal services in your community. There are volunteer lawyers in all states.

The Dove Project in New Hampshire provides legal representation to women, especially when the violent man has an attorney and the woman cannot afford one. Dove is sponsored by the New Hampshire Pro Bono Referral System in conjunction with the New Hampshire Coalition Against Domestic Violence and Sexual Abuse, and Women's Crisis Centers around the state.

The Domestic Violence Legal Clinic at the House of Ruth in Baltimore, Maryland, is one of the nation's few shelter-based legal clinics dedicated exclusively to the needs of abused women. This clinic provides legal remedies for custody and divorce as well as protective orders and other issues.

In New Mexico, the Domestic Violence Legal HELPline has an 800 number staffed by volunteer lawyers who will answer your questions weekdays from 9:00 A.M. to 5:00 P.M. This service is a project of the Center for Civic Values and the Young Lawyers Division of the State Bar of New Mexico.

If you hire your own attorney, you may be able to borrow enough money to make a down payment (retainer), start divorce proceedings, and work out installment payments for the balance as the case proceeds. Beware that divorce and custody cases can often drag on and exhaust your resources as well as those of a sole practitioner or small law firm. The emotional drain on you and your attorney may also be high, especially where courts are unresponsive to the risks posed by domestic violence.

Interviewing an Attorney

When you meet with the attorney, bring all the information that will be useful, such as protective orders, police and medical records, and photos of your injuries and property damage. If you will need maintenance and child support, bring a detailed budget of your expenses for rent, utilities, medical care, child care, transportation, and food. Bring copies of the most current bills for rent and utilities, as well as copies of pay stubs and tax returns—yours and his.

If you are still living with the abusive man, be sure to tell the attorney not to contact you at home. Ask that messages be left for you at your job or a safe place you designate. Be absolutely certain that the attorney has not put your real address and phone number on papers that get typed or filed by others in the office who may inadvertently mail things to you at home. Talk to the clerical staff yourself, and let them know the danger you face.

Attorneys might ask you to read and sign a statement of client's rights and responsibilities before they meet with you and agree to begin on your case. This is a summary of what the attorney can ask of you and what you should expect from the attorney in the way of fees, confidentiality, work, research, and auxiliary services such as the hiring of detectives. This statement of client rights might take an hour to read, but take it seriously. It is designed to protect you from unscrupulous or uncaring lawyers. It is the result of the efforts of a group of women who had gotten unfair divorces, banded together, and forced the system to change.

Some women like to bring a family member or friend with them when they interview an attorney. This gives them moral support at a time when they are highly stressed and might not be able to present their situation as thoroughly as possible. Although most attorneys will not object, keep in mind that when a third party is present, the attorney-client privilege is compromised. Be sure to ask your attorney exactly how this will affect your relationship.

Negotiating Realistically for Money and Property

Because violent men need to believe they have control over you, consider giving in on some issues so you can win the important ones. Don't let the emotional aspect of the relationship interfere with clear and rational thinking. With your attorney's help, try to make an unemotional and intelligent assessment of what's worth keeping and what you would be willing to give up.

Areas of negotiation that will surely come up are child custody and support, and visitation as well. In order to keep custody and have control of visitation so that you and your children are safe, you may need to give up some money or property. But bargain wisely—don't give everything away.

Unless you have been out of the workforce for a long time, you will probably not be able to get long-term maintenance—which used to be called alimony—from your abusive partner. But if you have children, you are entitled to child support, and if you have property in common with him, you are entitled to a portion of that as well. Many women are forced to leave their homes to escape violence, leaving everything behind with the abusive man. In the past the man could claim that because you left him and legally abandoned him, you left your property, too. Today, you have a better chance of getting what is rightfully yours.

Always get as much as possible of any financial and property settlement up front because there is no guarantee he will make payments over the long term. If you and your abusive partner had substantial holdings in stocks or property, your attorney might be able make arrangements for a payout over a longer period of time. But when there is no security for the future, this is not a good strategy. Ask your attorney about using a life insurance policy or a mortgage as collateral for maintenance and child support.

Keep a support system around you while you go through the divorce. You might be stunned by your husband's minimizing and denying the violence, even blaming you for it. If you go in knowing he will do this, you can be prepared. He may also be posturing to avoid paying you. For example, he may want you to sign away all property rights in exchange for custody of the children.

One woman was married to a self-employed fruit and vegetable vendor who routinely underreported his income. He also beat her and stuck a loaded gun in her mouth. They had been married less than eight months, and the woman was pregnant. The police arrested the man after the gun incident, but he claimed that because his business had suddenly taken a turn for the worse, he could not pay maintenance or child support. Fortunately, this woman had the foresight to make a copy of a diary her husband carried around to record all of his business transactions.

The diary showed a great deal of income, so the woman's attorney hired a private detective to follow this man and prove that he made enough money to support his wife and child.

Avoiding Joint Custody

Women usually got custody of the children in divorces until men started to object in the 1970s. The result was a backlash from men that led to awarding joint custody in most divorces. (In New York and some other states, joint custody would not be awarded if one parent was on trial.) This, of course, posed another dilemma. Because the court could not accept evidence of domestic violence in a no-fault divorce, it could not use such evidence to show the risk to children if the abusive father had custody.

In the mid-1990s, states began changing laws so courts would have to consider evidence of domestic violence to guide their decisions on child custody and visitation rights. Many states now require that the court consider domestic violence as contrary to the best interests of the child. Although the New Hampshire statutes contain a presumption that joint legal custody is in the best interest of children who are minors, the statute now also requires a court to consider family abuse as harmful to children. In Arizona joint custody is prohibited if a court finds significant domestic violence or enough evidence that there was a history of it. Before granting custody, the courts must consider all relevant factors, including findings from another court, police and medical records, child protective services records, domestic violence shelter records, school records, and witness testimony.

While joint custody might enhance equality of parenthood, children living under joint custody in high-conflict families are more emotionally troubled than those in the custody of only one parent.

Your Rights to Custody

Despite these legislative changes, there are occasions when violent men get custody of their children. There are also some states where mediation is required in custody cases. Mediation is designed to give parents an opportunity to negotiate their differences with the help of a trained neutral third party and avoid the adversarial system of the courtroom. However, this process is fraught with peril because mediators are not always well informed about domestic violence.

Some advocates believe that for mediation to work, the court should use a male and female mediation team and separate interviews of mother and father, allowing joint interviews only after a compromise is reached. In this way it might be possible to arrange a temporary visitation and custody agreement that could be changed if it proves unworkable.

In a custody hearing you will be asked for a history of the abuse and how it has affected your children. Be sure to report every incident, how and where your children were, what they said, how they reacted, how they are doing in school, everything. Remember all the evidence you have been accumulating! If you have been keeping a diary of the abuse, recording dates and times, you can read from that.

Psychological evaluations are often required before determining custody. It is critical that there be evaluations of both parents by a therapist with experience in domestic violence. The therapist should be a social worker, psychologist, or psychiatrist. Be sure to get advice from your attorney and/or domestic violence advocate. You are under great stress, trying to protect your children, fearing their loss. You might be jumpy, nervous, and tearful. Or you might appear cold and calculating because you are trying so hard to keep your emotions under control and project quiet strength. Your abuser, on the other hand, might appear poised, well-spoken, and perfectly fit. You might be subject to evaluation about your ability to develop independent goals, free yourself from feelings of guilt, use a community support network, and disengage from the abusive partner.

One judge explained that it was the mother's agitated and anxiety-riddled courtroom behavior that convinced him that it would be better for the women to "get relief from child care for a while so she could pull herself together." In another case a man had beaten his wife so severely that she was in the hospital, but he was awarded temporary custody of the children, even though there was an aunt who was willing to care for them. The judge said the rights of the father took precedence over the rights of the children, even though the kids were terrified of the father.

In Louisiana the court cannot deny you custody because you were physically or emotionally damaged by the abuse. In Kentucky you cannot be charged with abandoning the family home if you left because you were seriously threatened with bodily harm. In Michigan courts cannot use your temporary residence in a shelter as evidence that you tried to conceal the children from the abuser. Fleeing to shelter is not abandonment or parental negligence. In California, if you stay at a shelter or at another confidential location, the court must design custody and visitation orders that prevent disclosure of its location. Missouri authorizes the court to delete the address of the custodial parent or child from any reports or records made available to the abuser.

Also remember that his problems are chronic and that yours are not. He cannot stop being violent, and even if he finally loosens his grip on you, he will find another woman and do the same thing to her. You, on the other hand, will be more stable once you are away from him. You have a much a better chance of overcoming any psychological trauma and fulfilling your role as a parent.

Ironically, more women are injured by domestic violence than from rapes, muggings, and auto accidents combined. And the risk increases when women leave the relationship. However, if you don't leave and your children are abused by your partner, then you can be prosecuted—and sent to jail—as an accomplice to child abuse. Yet if you leave, you may be killed. Never forget that our legal and judicial system was established by men for men. The number of female attorneys and judges and district attorneys is growing, but they are still greatly outnumbered by the men.

Don't risk your children's lives or your own for lack of competent legal help. It is available, no matter what your financial circumstances.

Getting Child Support

Whether you are married or not, your state has child support laws that require the noncustodial parent to pay a certain amount to support the children. Most states have a formula for the assignment of child support. It is a sliding scale according to number of children and the combined income of the parents. For example, if you earn $16,000 and he earns $40,000, he will have to pay a larger share.

Laws about child support are becoming more strict; in most states if the father does not pay, he goes to jail. The court's probation office will track him down if he tries to flee, although this does not always work because of staff shortages. If the man is unlucky enough to live in Quincy, Massachusetts, however, his picture might appear in the newspaper, and somebody will recognize him and turn him in.

Negotiate Visitation with Safety in Mind

If the father of your children does not get custody of his children, he will almost always be granted "reasonable rights" of visitation unless he has physically abused the children and you can prove it. A child's need for protection from mental and physical harm must be balanced with the child's need to maintain a relationship with both parents, so the court will allow both of you to figure out "reasonable" visitation.

In some states an abusive man must prove to the court that visitation will not endanger his child physically or emotionally. If you are in New Jersey, ask the court for a Visitation Risk Assessment Interview Sheet to help you plan visitation or to convince a judge not to grant it at all. Other states may have this by now. This is used by court staff before any award of visitation is made, but you might need to ask for it.

If you want supervised visitation, the court might ask you to design the plan yourself. Do this with the safety of your children and yourself in mind.

Many women are hurt when a violent man comes to pick up his children, and the children can become pawns in this struggle. So arrange for your partner to pick up the children and return them to the home of a close family member or friend, or arrange for someone to be present at your home during these times. This way you won't have to be confronted by the abusive man. Keep your attorney and counselor/advocate informed of any problems with exchange and transfer of children. And most important, teach your children a safety plan (see the previous chapter) for when they visit with their father.

It's also a good idea to keep a diary of all contacts relating to exchange and transfer of children, especially any threatening incidents. It is common for courts to adjust visitation rulings even with one such incident. If visitation rules are spelled out in the protective order, let the police or court know if there is a violation.

Protecting Your Children's Rights

Ask your attorney and the court if they will help you draw up a contract between your children and their father, or have the court enter an order defining the limits of visitation. (Some judges will not consider preferences of very young children.) The contract might include your child's rights to contact you or an advocate by phone at any time during the visit with their father. The attorney Barbara Hart, legal director of the Pennsylvania Coalition Against Domestic Violence, suggests that such a contract outline the responsibilities of the father and any limitations on his liberties. It should reflect the child's preferences and incorporate safety measures. For example, the father must

- agree not to use drugs or alcohol during the visit
- ask no questions about you
- take your child to planned activities
- return all your child's clothing and personal possessions taken during the visit
- remove weapons from the house during the visit
- pick up your child at a specified location other than your home

The contract might include some backup clauses that describe your child's rights in the event of the father's violation. For example, if the father becomes drunk, your child might have the right to leave and return to you. If these terms are included in a custody order and your child calls you to say her father is drunk, you might be able to get the police to help pick up your child.

State Visitation Centers

In some states there are visitation centers where a man can visit or pick up his children under supervision, so that there is no contact between the parents.

Such supervision is also available for on-site visitation when it is believed that the parents cannot maintain a peaceful setting.

In Delaware, for example, the Division of State Service Centers operates Family Visitation Centers, a neutral and safe place for violent parents to visit their children. These centers provide a safe setting where a child can maintain or reestablish a relationship with a father. At the same time you can feel reassured that your child will be protected and that you do not need to confront the man. Fees are generally based upon the ability to pay, but victims of domestic violence are not responsible for payment.

The Children's Safety Center in Duluth, Minnesota, is open one weekday, one weekend day, and one evening of each week, and it is designed to accommodate parents who are unable to control hostility during pickup and return of children. Here you would have no contact with the abuser, as both of you arrive and leave by different entrances and exits. You can stay at the site or leave. Before gaining access to this center, you and your abusive partner are interviewed by the program coordinator to get a history of the violence. Visitation times are arranged and rules of conduct explained. The center provides a variety of children's books, games, and videotapes, as well as beverages and snacks for children and adults. The noncustodial parent is strongly urged to participate in parenting classes.

Separating Your Children from the Abuser

When a relationship ends, children often blame themselves, especially in violent homes, where the arguments that started the fights may have involved them; in some cases the children might have been obliged to telephone the police or intervene directly. Children do not always need a reason to blame themselves, so you might want to help them express their thoughts about leaving. If your local domestic violence advocates have programs for children, this may be a good time to seek them out. This is also a time to talk with counselors in your child's school.

Be honest with your children. Tell them that it was hard to leave before because you hoped the violence would stop. And it does not mean that you do not love their father. It just means you realize that the violence will not stop and that you can no longer tolerate such violence. It is not safe for them or for you. If you have left in the past and returned, it is important to let them know that this time you mean to stay away.

Explain how the custody process works, and let them know they will be able to see their father if they want to, but only if it is safe. If you will not let them see him until you are assured of their safety and your own, explain why. Discuss the court order and its meaning.

Tell them that you are still a family but will be living as a different kind of family now. Let them know that others are helping you to make this transition.

CHAPTER 11

How to Begin Building a Life without Violence

The Women's Center and Shelter of Pittsburgh followed up with women who had been served by the shelter and found that the majority of residential and nonresidential women who had been counseled by shelter staff were in violence-free homes one year after the intervention.

The second biggest obstacle to leaving a violent relationship—after fear of retaliation from an abusive partner—is lack of money. Even if you already have a job, you may not be able to survive on only one paycheck. Most families today need two. Leaving your abuser can have a profoundly negative effect on your standard of living. According to the National Woman Abuse Prevention Project, in the first year after divorce, a woman's standard of living drops by 73 percent, while a man's improves by 42 percent.

If you have been dependent upon your abuser for financial support, you may find it more difficult to break free, but there are many ways to get help in establishing your short- and long-term independence. If you have dependent children, the road will be tougher, but with help from the resources available, it can be done. In the beginning you may feel discouraged or demoralized at having to be dependent on your family, friends, and people you don't know very well in the state and local social service agencies. Nevertheless, you eventually get through it and come out on the other side in a more optimistic frame of mind. Keep your goal in mind. This is part of the process. This is a time when friends, relatives, shelter workers, and advocates can help you with practical matters and emotional support.

Emergency Public Assistance

In some communities any victim of domestic violence, regardless of income, is entitled to emergency services, including shelter and emergency cash. A domestic violence coalition or shelter in your community can often help you get such emergency services and help you apply for assistance in order to survive on your own. Emergency assistance can pay for storing your furniture and other belongings. It can pay for moving expenses, rent, security deposit, brokers and finders fees, and household items needed to start a new home. If you were forced to leave your home and have no money on hand to feed yourself and your family, the domestic violence center or shelter may be able to help you get "expedited" service for food stamps. This means you will get them within a few days, rather than a few weeks, of your application. This kind of assistance could last for up to six months after the emergency.

If you have a job but your salary does not cover your necessary expenses such as rent, food, medical needs, and child support, you may qualify for public assistance to make up the difference, depending upon the regulations in your state. In most cases it takes four to six weeks to establish eligibility and receive payments.

Your community may have other sources of emergency food furnishings such as charitable organizations. Ask your advocate about this.

When You Apply for Help

When you go to the human or social services agency to apply for benefits, bring relevant records, including your protective order. If you don't want the abusive man to find you, be firm about reminding them not to divulge your new address and phone number to anyone.

To prove your emergency status, you may need proof of the violence, such as testimony from a friend or neighbor; police, court, or hospital records; or a letter from a shelter worker. Bring other necessary documents, such as children's birth certificates, marriage and/or divorce records, social security numbers, rent receipts, and utility bills. You might also need your children's school records and your own medical records if you are dependent upon medication or treatment of any kind.

If the agency people tell you they must first find out if your abuser is supporting you or the children, it will take time for them to check up on your abusive partner. But in the meantime, you need food and money for rent. Tell them that a violent incident forced you to leave home or that he left you and you therefore have no money from him. Ask for a "good cause exception."

If you are age sixty-five or over, there may be additional forms of assistance from agencies such as the Office of the Aging in your community. You might qualify for rent subsidies, job training, and discounts on utilities and transportation.

If you are an immigrant—legal or illegal—ask your domestic violence advocate how changes in the welfare laws in 1996 affect your eligibility for benefits in your state.

Go to the social service agency early in the morning to apply. Always fill out the paperwork at the agency even if you cannot complete all of it. Speed is of the essence in getting through the bureaucracy. Even if someone tells you they do not think you are eligible, file anyway, and follow up. You might need rent receipts and copies of utility bills. Always get the names of the caseworkers you talk with.

If you are denied benefits even though you believe you are eligible, make an appointment at the legal aid office nearest you, and call your domestic violence advocate for advice.

Collecting Child Support Payments

Child support can be mandated through a protective order or through a legal separation, divorce, or child custody motion. The terms of an order of protection can outline costs your abuser must pay during the life of the order. This can include not only child support, but also out-of-pocket medical expenses, food, rent, and other necessities. If the father of your children is ordered to pay child support and he fails to do so, the money can be withheld from his paycheck. This is now law in most states.

If you are receiving public assistance, the welfare bureau might instigate a child support action against the father for you through the support enforcement office. If you have an order from a court and your abusive partner fails to pay child support, the welfare office can go to court for you. In some states, these payments, when collected, are made directly to the welfare office and held for you.

Suing for Damages

You are also entitled to file a suit against your abusive partner for damages such as lost wages, medical expenses, and property damage. Ask your domestic violence advocates or call your local bar association for advice on how to do this. In some communities you can make such demands part of a protective order. Your abuser can be ordered to pay for injuries and damages as well as a designated amount for "pain and suffering."

A lawsuit can take a longer time, but your abusive partner might be willing to make a quick settlement if there is enough pressure on him. Talk with a lawyer about this.

Crime Victim's Compensation

You might also be eligible for compensation from the Crime Victim's Compensation Fund if you have suffered physically or emotionally because of a violent crime. This fund is a secondary source that pays for certain out-of-pocket expenses related to the crime that you have no other way to pay. Ask your domestic violence advocates about this, or call the state attorney general's office in your county.

You might be required to live separately from the abuser when you file a notice of intent and when the compensation is awarded. To qualify, you must report the crime to a law enforcement agency within seventy-two hours (unless you are under eighteen and there is a good reason why the crime was not reported during this time). In some states you must file criminal charges against the abuser. Under this program you can be compensated for some of the following:

- reasonable medical, prescription, and rehabilitation expenses
- mental health counseling
- loss of earnings or support
- child care so you can go to work
- reasonable attorney fees for assistance with the claim
- reasonable costs associated with crime scene cleanup
- reasonable replacement costs for clothing or bedding taken as evidence or made unusable as a result of the criminal investigation

Applications for the Crime Victim's Compensation Fund are available from police, hospitals, and the courts.

Defense Department Program

If you or your abusive partner is in the military, you might qualify for funds from Transitional Compensation for Abused Family Members. These funds can be awarded to you if your abusive partner is convicted of a criminal offense against you. The Department of Defense makes this fund available to all branches of the military.

Finding More Work

In this age of downsizing, getting a job is not easy. You might already have a job and need a second job to make ends meet. Some domestic violence shelters have job training and employment placement programs, or they work in conjunction with such programs. You might want to apply for a job with some of the companies listed in chapter 8, which are concerned about domestic violence. Here are some other avenues to explore:

- Unemployment insurance. If you were working, and forced to leave your job because of your partner's violence, you may be eligible for unemployment compensation.
- Displaced homemaker programs, such as the Illinois Network for Displaced Homemakers. Some states have a variety of job search skills and counseling services. To help homemakers become successful in the paid workforce, they may offer job search skills, counseling, referral, education and training, job development and placement. Call your state department of employment for information.
- Community groups such as the YWCA, Commu-

nity Action Agencies, Urban League, Career Guidance Centers, and others often sponsor job training or placement programs.

- Job Opportunities in Nevada (JOIN) is a federally funded program that provides career counseling, employment workshops, classroom skills training, and on-the-job training and placement. That state also has a CEP program (Claimant Employment Project), which helps unemployment claimants return to work sooner by providing classroom and on-the-job training.

- Temporary employment agencies can help you through a transition so that you work only the days you wish and are thus free to go to court. This is a way to get a job quickly, because it is not a long-term employment contract.

- Some unions have apprentice programs. You might sign up for a nontraditional job such as plumber or electrician. While you work as an apprentice, you are earning money and covered by benefits. Once you go through the apprenticeship, you earn union scale.

- Take civil service tests.

Paying for Medical Care

State laws vary on Medicare, Medicaid, and other forms of public health assistance. In some areas your medical bills for the previous three months, before application, might be covered. Apply for Medicaid if you think you are eligible.

Some communities, like Quincy, Massachusetts, provide free health care for women and children from violent homes. This is the exception, but ask domestic violence advocates about health care. There may be other programs where you can get affordable medical care.

If you are insured under a health plan as a dependent with your abusive partner, you can continue that coverage under the terms of a protective order. If you and your children have moved to a new home in a confidential location, using the insurance might reveal your whereabouts. Ask domestic violence advocates for advice, or call the health care provider and find out if any paperwork will be sent to you. Explain that the terms of your protective order include continuing coverage on his medical insurance policy but that he is not permitted to come near your home. You may need the court to work it out.

Finding a New Home

Single-parent households spend an average of 59 percent of household income on rent. For female-headed households with children, the rent burden is even worse. Since 1974 the percentage of female-headed households paying more than 75 percent of their income for rent has doubled (from 17 to 34 percent).

If you cannot keep the home you shared because he will not leave, your name is not on the lease, or you simply do not feel safe there, then you must find your own place, move in with relatives, or find shared housing.

Finding an inexpensive home can be difficult for everybody, not just women leaving abusive relationships. It will take perseverance, persistence, and the ability to withstand constant frustration. Start by telling everyone you know that you are looking for a home. Check the classified sections of all of your daily and weekly newspapers. Call real-estate brokers. Post a notice at the women's shelter or domestic violence center.

If you are receiving public assistance, ask your caseworker about publicly subsidized housing. You may qualify for Section 8 Housing, which is subsidized by the federal government. In this program part of the rent is paid by you and part by the government. The waiting list is several years long, but women getting away from domestic violence go to the top of the list. Check with your local rent assistance agency or public housing authority.

What to Look for in a New Home

Put security on top of the list of what to look for when you are scouting out a new home. Check windows, doors, locks, and access. Check out the neighborhood. Is the street well lighted at night? Or is it the kind of street where a stalker could lurk unnoticed? Are there stores and neighbors nearby in case you need to get help?

In addition to asking what the rent and utilities cost, here are some more things to find out:

- How safe is the building?
- Is there regular maintenance?
- Can you install extra locks for safety?
- Are there restrictions about children or pets?
- Are there smoke detectors?
- Is the building superintendent on the premises?
- Are the front-door locks secure?
- Are there safety bars on upper floors to protect children?

Tenant laws are very strong in some cities and almost nonexistent in others. Before you sign a lease, read it carefully and question anything you do not understand. Make them aware that you know what standards should be. Refer to chapter 7 about keeping your home safe.

Shared Housing

You may decided to live with relatives or friends until you find a new home. Or you may find someone at the women's shelter to share a home with. One woman and her two children moved in with another woman and her three children. They were able to rent a big, inexpensive house in a pleasant city neighborhood because the building was scheduled to be torn down in a few years to make way for a housing development and the landlord did not care how many children were there. The house was not in the best of shape, but it was safe, habitable, and roomy. The two women were able to live there for two years. One worked nights as a registered nurse and the other days as a reporter, so one was always home to care for the children, all five of whom were between the ages of five and eight.

The Dove program in Quincy, Massachusetts, provides transitional living through Cilla's House. Three families share low-income housing for up to a year while they regain independence and work toward self-sufficiency. Women in the program pay 30 percent of their income for rent while Dove supplements the remainder and provides utilities, phone service, and an alarm system for safety. Residents are chosen from women in local shelters, and those attending Dove's community domestic violence support groups. The staff provides counseling and advocacy, easing the transition into school or work. They offer residents budgeting assistance, access to community resources, and, most importantly, long-term support and stabilization.

If you let people know what you want to do, you might find unexpected ways to make it work.

Getting the Emotional Support You Need

Most women's centers and shelters have support groups for residents and nonresidents in abusive relationships. Because you are in a group with other women who have the same experience, you will not feel intimidated or isolated. These women know exactly what you are talking about and they can offer compassion and understanding as well as hard practical advice.

In a support group you are free to talk or not to talk. You may want to just sit in for a few weeks. More than half the women who are abused never tell anyone about it, according to a poll by Louis Harris & Associates. Those who are willing to talk usually prefer their own support network of family or friends. But women going through the same experience are like family. You will feel a strong bond with them.

You might be more inhibited than others, but you will be accepted. Here you do not have to keep anything a secret or hide behind a facade of domestic bliss or pretend nothing is wrong. You can express your anger, shed your tears, and get a hug. This is a good place to gather strength and make plans to leave the abusive relationship. You will learn that the men in other women's lives did and said the same things, made the same promises to stop. You'll learn that violent men may look different, but their problem is the same.

It is important for you to talk with other women, to see that there is a life after domestic violence. Hearing stories from women who have been through the same thing will give you ideas about how to help yourself. You will find out how other women coped with paying rent, finding a new home, going to court, and keeping themselves safe.

YOUR FAMILY AND FRIENDS

If you have a warm, supportive family who can help you without judging you or overprotecting you, then you are lucky. Otherwise think carefully before you enlist their help or move in with them. Depending upon the reactions and attitudes, your situation could be very frustrating. For instance, if you kept the violence a secret and now tell them you are leaving because your man beat you up, they may not believe you. They may not be well informed about domestic violence. They may prefer denial, or disapprove and tell you that it is wrong to break up a family.

Then there's the other extreme. Your family and friends may accuse you of being an idiot for staying in such a relationship for so long. Few people really understand the complexities of love and fear and how dangerous it is to leave an abusive man. People like to blame the victim. "Why don't you just leave?" is a very common question. If you are surrounded by people with this attitude, it will make you feel so bad about yourself that you will be tempted to return home to your abuser. Avoid this at all costs. You need support now, not criticism. When you have recovered and feel stronger, then you can explain to them what it was really like.

An overprotective family that takes you in and then refuses to let you be independent is also a problem. They control you, like the violent man did. This could be stifling.

If you have been kept isolated by your domestic situation, it may be difficult for you to suddenly become a dynamic extrovert, but it is important to end the isolation and seek out new friends. Think about all the people you know and would like to know better. Look for supportive, nonjudgmental people. You might find women at the shelter, or there might be somebody at work you'd like to know better. If you begin to live the way you choose and do the things you enjoy, you will begin to meet new people.

Perhaps you can get to know mothers of your children's friends. Perhaps you held back before because you were embarrassed about the violence. If you have been working with domestic violence advocates and women at the shelters, you have already witnessed the power of community.

INDIVIDUAL COUNSELING

If you have been in an abusive relationship for a long time, you have many deep wounds to heal, and you might benefit from one-on-one counseling with a qualified therapist experienced in treating women in abusive relationships. A professional therapist can guide you past the fears, denial, and depression—all the things that you worry about. You might be lonely and frightened, afraid to trust any man again.

There are many kinds of psychological and emotional therapy, and your first call should be to your local shelter or the domestic violence coalition in your state. They are connected to a network of services, including individual therapy with a psychologist, psychiatrist, social worker, or paraprofessional. All have professional credentials, but fees are the highest with a psychiatrist who is also a medical doctor. A psychologist is most commonly a Ph.D., while a social worker has a master's degree. The degree, at least initially, might be less important than their experience with domestic violence. The paraprofessional may not have comprehensive education in therapy but may be especially well trained in the particular area you need right now, so consider all of them. These therapists are usually found at crisis intervention centers and shelters. States require licenses to practice, and medical insurance reimbursement often depends on that.

You will probably feel better talking with a woman

at this time. If you have been abused for a long time by a man, it may not be easy to talk openly to a male therapist right now. Write a list of questions you want to ask of a therapist, such as the following:

- What is your fee?
- What special training do you have with domestic violence?
- How many women with my background have you treated?
- Are appointments available days or evenings?
- What kind of credentials and degrees do you have?

You may need to see a few therapists before you find one you feel comfortable with. After you talk with them in person or on the phone, let your impressions come through. Is she sympathetic and knowledgeable about domestic violence? Is she warm and friendly or businesslike, concerned or indifferent? Your emotions are fragile right now, but you will have a sense of the person you would be willing to trust. Let your instincts guide you once you have done the research and know what you need. Avoid any therapist who suggests you need marriage counseling or that you need therapy focused on you as a codependent personality.

Ask about the goals of therapy. How much time will it take to deal with the immediate crisis, how much time to help you plan a new life, what are the expectations, and so on. Therapy and counseling should be helpful to you over a period of several months; you can always continue the treatment for a longer period if you want, but make it clear that you are looking for short-term solutions to help you change your life.

Remember, you are the client, and you pay for the counseling, even if the money is coming from your health insurance or a public assistance program. You are responsible for using your money wisely to get the best help you can. Some medical insurance covers counseling for domestic violence. Sometimes it will cover costs for specific illnesses such as clinical depression or schizophrenia, but it will not cover crisis intervention.

GETTING STRONG

While taking care of your emotional needs, you will feel more like taking care of your body as well. Years of physical and emotional abuse can leave you physically and emotionally weak. Your body is a mass of tension. You may have a variety of serious and minor ailments as a result—not only injuries, but also chronic physical conditions such as hypertension, gastrointestinal disorders, gynecological problems, migraine headaches, and clinical depression. You need to restore your body and your soul. Ask your doctor about proper nutrition, and get a complete physical exam so you can take care of any physical problems and get better. Refer back to chapter 5 for information on dealing with the health care system.

Physical exercise is a great way to release the tensions of anger and anxiety, certainly much better than the way your abusive partner released his anger. It's a great way to lift your spirits. When you are in motion, your body's natural opiates—endorphins— are released. These are the body's natural feel-good hormones. Our bodies are more efficient when we exercise regularly. Lift weights to develop strength, do aerobics to develop endurance. You might even consider a self-defense class such as karate.

Look in the mirror and see a strong, competent person.

SERENITY AND SANCTUARY

Whether you are now in your own house or apartment, or sharing cramped quarters with other people, you need a place that is just for you, a place where you will not be interrupted by the violence, by the terrified cries of your children screaming for help, by an abusive man throwing the dishes against the wall. You need a refuge where your thoughts are not shattered by the sudden burst of violence or abuse. When you are hypervigilant it is like being in the front lines of a war. It takes the same toll on your body and your psyche. You need a place where you can just relax and let go of your anxiety.

If you want to lie around, read romance novels for

a few hours, or talk with a friend on the phone, then give yourself permission to do this. You need to learn how to live without the constant worry about something setting off a violent episode. The longer you live away from it and the more you strengthen yourself with support from others, the more you will enjoy yourself.

Make your home, even your temporary surroundings, as much your own as you can. Create the kind of environment where you can feel calm and at peace. If this is not possible in the house, then find a place that is uniquely your own. Perhaps you like to visit the library and just sit and read there, where it is quiet. Maybe you have a favorite beach or shorefront or spot in the park. Go to a museum and sit in front of a wonderful picture you like. Sit inside a particularly beautiful church. Sanctuary could be treating yourself to a cappuccino at your favorite coffee shop or going to a movie. Music is a great healer if you are lucky enough to have a sound system—just sit and listen.

If you are still in the home you shared with a violent man, and you have made it safe (refer to chapter 7), now make it yours. Remove all of his things from view until he sends for them. Rearrange the house so you don't look at empty spaces where his jacket used to hang or his coffee mug used to be. Put your own things in their place. Paint the walls a new color, rearrange the furniture, make it truly your home.

Most women have no trouble adapting to the peace and quiet. Domestic violence is gone. Domestic bliss is now a real possibility in your life.

It may take many tries before you can leave the abuser and stay away for good, but despite setbacks and retaliations, if you keep trying and get the kind of help you need, it will eventually work. Each time you make an inquiry, make a call, report abuse to police, or seek medical or emotional help, you get stronger.

Love may have turned violent, and you will grieve for the love that never became what you had hoped it would be. Eventually, you can let it go and move on to a more centered and focused life, built on the foundation of your own strength.

You are strong.

You are free.

You can do anything.

What's Available in Your Community

A State-by-State Guide to Resources

By calling the domestic violence coalition in your state, you can find out what you need to know about your local area. The first state coalition against domestic violence was established in Pennsylvania in 1976. Now every state has a central organization devoted to helping abused women through referrals, lobbying, and education. These coalitions are networks with access to resources throughout the state. Some offer comprehensive help such as detailed handbooks—in English and other languages—as well as referrals to shelters, financial assistance, counseling programs, and help for children. Some have twenty-four-hour statewide crisis or information telephone numbers. These hot lines are available in every state—either statewide or regionally.

You can call any of the coalitions without giving your name if you want to protect your privacy and safety. Some will accept collect calls. They can help you find counseling, medical clinics, shelters, safe houses, support groups, mental health services, human service agencies, legal services, victim assistance programs, and police domestic violence officers.

Studies show that the more options you have, the more likely you will be to seek outside help to end the violence in your life and leave your abusive partner. Community intervention varies considerably from state to state, but all states have programs to help you get away from an abusive relationship.

If your state has only local telephone hot lines that cover certain countries or cities, you can get the number you need from your state coalition or your telephone information operator. Many coalitions also have E-mail addresses. This is a good way to get information if you are shy about asking by phone and if you do not want mail from such an organization coming to your home.

If you cannot reach your state coalition, call the federal domestic violence hot line at 800–799–SAFE (7233) or 800–787–3224.

Remember, if you are in immediate danger, always call 911.

THE ALABAMA COALITION AGAINST DOMESTIC
VIOLENCE
P.O. Box 4762
Montgomery, AL 36101
334–832–4842 (local hot lines only)

ALASKA NETWORK ON DOMESTIC VIOLENCE AND
SEXUAL ASSAULT
130 Seward Street, No. 501
Juneau, Alaska 99801
907–586–3650 (local hot lines)

ARIZONA COALITION AGAINST DOMESTIC VIOLENCE
100 West Camelback, Suite 109
Phoenix, AZ 85013
602–279–2900
Statewide 24-hour crisis hot line: 800–786–7380
(800–STOP–DV–0)
Statewide information hot line: 800–782–6400

ARKANSAS COALITION AGAINST DOMESTIC VIOLENCE
523 S. Louisiana, Suite 230
Little Rock, AR 72201
501–399–9486 (local hot lines only)

CALIFORNIA ALLIANCE AGAINST DOMESTIC VIOLENCE
Modesto, CA 95354
209–524–1888
Statewide hot line: 800–877–3945

COLORADO DOMESTIC VIOLENCE COALITION
P.O. Box 18902
Denver, CO 80218
303–573–9018
303–573–7814 (local hot lines only)

CONNECTICUT COALITION AGAINST DOMESTIC
VIOLENCE
135 Broad Street
Hartford, CT 06105
860–524–5890 (local hot lines only)

DELAWARE COALITION AGAINST DOMESTIC VIOLENCE
P.O. Box 847
Wilmington, DE 19899
302–658–2958
Statewide hot line: 800–701–0456

DISTRICT OF COLUMBIA COALITION AGAINST DOMESTIC
VIOLENCE
513 U Street, N.W.
Washington, DC 20013
202–387–5630 (local hot lines only)

FLORIDA COALITION AGAINST DOMESTIC VIOLENCE
1535-C5 Killearn Center Boulevard
Tallahassee, FL 32308
904–668–6862
Statewide hot line: 800–500–1119; 800–621–4202

GEORGIA COALITION ON FAMILY VIOLENCE, INC.
1827 Powers Ferry Road
Building 3, Suite 25
Atlanta, GA 30339
770–984–0085 (local hot lines only)

HAWAII STATE COALITION AGAINST DOMESTIC
VIOLENCE
98–939 Moanalua Road
Aiea, HI 96701–5012
808–486–5072 (local hot lines only)

IDAHO COALITION AGAINST SEXUAL AND DOMESTIC
VIOLENCE
200 North Fourth Street, Suite 10-K
Boise, ID 83702
208–384–0419
Statewide hot line: 800–669–3176

ILLINOIS COALITION AGAINST DOMESTIC VIOLENCE
730 East Vine Street, Room 109
Springfield, IL 62703
217–789–2830 (local hot lines only)

INDIANA COALITION AGAINST DOMESTIC VIOLENCE
2511 E. 46th St., Suite N–3
Indianapolis, IN 46205
317–543–3908
Statewide hot line: 800–332–7385

IOWA COALITION AGAINST DOMESTIC VIOLENCE
1504 High Street, Suite 100
Des Moines, Iowa 50309–3123
515–244–8028
Statewide hot line: 800–942–0333

KANSAS COALITION AGAINST SEXUAL AND DOMESTIC
VIOLENCE
820 S.E. Quincy, Suite 416
Topeka, KS 66612
913–232–9784
Statewide hot line: 800–400–8864

KENTUCKY DOMESTIC VIOLENCE ASSOCIATION
P.O. Box 356
Frankfort, KY 40602
502–875–4132 (local hot lines only)

LOUISIANA COALITION AGAINST DOMESTIC VIOLENCE
P.O. Box 3053
Hammond, LA 70404–3053
504–542–6561 (local hot lines only)

MAINE COALITION FOR FAMILY CRISIS SERVICES
128 Main Street
Bangor, ME 04401
207–941–1194 (local hot lines only)

MARYLAND NETWORK AGAINST DOMESTIC
VIOLENCE
11501 Georgia Avenue
Suite 403
Silver Spring, MD 20902–1955
301–942–0900
Statewide hot line: 800–634–3577

MASSACHUSETTS COALITION OF BATTERED WOMEN
SERVICE GROUPS
14 Beacon Street, Suite 507
Boston, MA 02108
617–248–0922 (local hot lines only)

MICHIGAN COALITION AGAINST DOMESTIC
VIOLENCE
P.O. Box 16009
Lansing, MI 48901
517–887–9334
Statewide hot line: 800–99–NO–ABUSE
(800–662–2873)

MINNESOTA COALITION FOR BATTERED WOMEN
450 N. Syndicate St., Suite 122
St. Paul, MN 55104
612–646–6177, voice and TDD
Statewide hot line: 800–646–0994

MISSISSIPPI STATE COALITION AGAINST DOMESTIC
VIOLENCE
P.O. Box 4703
Jackson, MS 39296–4703
601–981–9196
Statewide hot line: 800–898–3234

MISSOURI COALITION AGAINST DOMESTIC VIOLENCE
331 Madison Street
Jefferson City, MO 65101
314–634–4161 (local hot lines only)

MONTANA COALITION AGAINST DOMESTIC VIOLENCE
P.O. Box 633
Helena, MT 59624
406–443–7794
Statewide hot line: 800–655–7867

NEBRASKA DOMESTIC VIOLENCE SEXUAL ASSAULT
COALITION
315 South 9th Street, Suite 18
Lincoln, NE 68508–2253
402–476–6256
Statewide hot line: 800–876–6238

THE NEVADA NETWORK AGAINST DOMESTIC
VIOLENCE
2100 Capurro Way, Suite E
Sparks, NV 89431

702–358–1171
702–358–0546
Statewide crisis hot line: 800–500–1556
Statewide information hot line: 800–230–1955

NEW HAMPSHIRE COALITION AGAINST DOMESTIC
VIOLENCE
P.O. Box 353
Concord, NH 03302–0353
603–224–8893
Statewide hot line: 800–852–3388

NEW JERSEY COALITION FOR BATTERED WOMEN
2620 Whitehorse-Hamilton Square Road
Trenton, NJ 08690
609–584–8107
Statewide hot line: 800–572–7233

NEW MEXICO COALITION AGAINST DOMESTIC VIOLENCE
P.O. Box 25363
Albuquerque, NM 87125
505–246–9240; 505–247–4219
Statewide hot line: 800–773–3645

THE NEW YORK STATE COALITION AGAINST DOMESTIC
VIOLENCE
The Women's Building
79 Central Avenue
Albany, NY 12206

518–432–4864
Statewide hot line: 800–942–6906; Español,
800–952–6908 (7:00 A.M. to 11:00 P.M.)

NORTH CAROLINA COALITION AGAINST DOMESTIC
VIOLENCE
P.O. Box 51875
Durham, NC 27717–1875
919–956–9124 (local hot lines only)

NORTH DAKOTA COUNCIL ON ABUSED WOMEN'S
SERVICE AND COALITION AGAINST SEXUAL ASSAULT
418 East Rosser, No. 320
Bismarck, ND 58501
701–255–6240
Statewide information hot line: 800–472–2911

OHIO DOMESTIC VIOLENCE NETWORK
4041 North High Street, Suite 101
Columbus, OH 43214
614–784–0023
Statewide hot line: 800–934–9840

OKLAHOMA COALITION AGAINST DOMESTIC VIOLENCE
AND SEXUAL ASSAULT
2200 N. Classen Blvd., Suite 610
Oklahoma City, OK 73106
405–557–1210 (local hot lines only)

OREGON COALITION AGAINST DOMESTIC AND SEXUAL
VIOLENCE
520 NW Davis, Suite 510
Portland, OR 97209
503–223–7411 (local hot lines only)

PENNSYLVANIA COALITION AGAINST DOMESTIC VIOLENCE
6400 Flank Drive, Suite 1300
Harrisburg, PA 17112–2778
717–671–4767 or 717–545–6400 (local hot lines only)

RHODE ISLAND COALITION AGAINST DOMESTIC VIOLENCE
422 Post Road, Suite 104
Warwick, RI 02888
401–467–9940
Statewide hot line: 800–494–8100

SOUTH CAROLINA COALITION AGAINST DOMESTIC
VIOLENCE AND SEXUAL ASSAULT
P.O. Box 7776
Columbia, SC 29202–7776
803–750–1222; 803–254–3699
Statewide hot line: 800–260–9293

SOUTH DAKOTA COALITION AGAINST DOMESTIC
VIOLENCE AND SEXUAL ASSAULT
P.O. Box 141
Pierre, SD 57501

605–945–0869
Statewide hot line: 800–430–7233

TENNESSEE TASK FORCE AGAINST DOMESTIC
VIOLENCE
P.O. Box 120972
Nashville, TN 37212
615–386–9406
Statewide hot line: 800–356–6767

TEXAS COUNCIL ON FAMILY VIOLENCE
8701 North Mopac Expressway, Suite 450
Austin, TX 78759
512–794–1133
Statewide hot line: 800–525–1978

UTAH DOMESTIC VIOLENCE ADVISORY COUNCIL
120 North 200 West, 2nd floor
Salt Lake City, UT 84103
801–538–4100
Statewide hot line: 800–897–LINK (5465);
weekdays 8:30 A.M. to 5:00 P.M.

VERMONT NETWORK AGAINST DOMESTIC VIOLENCE
AND SEXUAL ASSAULT
P.O. Box 405
Montpelier, VT 05601
802–223–1302
Statewide crisis hot line: 800–228–7395 (domestic
violence); 800–489–7273 (sexual assault)

VIRGINIANS AGAINST DOMESTIC VIOLENCE
2850 Sandy Bay Rd., Suite 101
Williamsburg, VA 23185–2362
804–221–0990
Statewide hot line: 800–838–8238

WASHINGTON STATE COALITION AGAINST DOMESTIC
VIOLENCE
2101 Fourth Avenue East, Suite 103
Olympia, WA 98506
360–352–4029
Statewide hot line: 800–562–6025

WEST VIRGINIA COALITION AGAINST DOMESTIC VIOLENCE
P.O. Box 85
181-B Main Street
Sutton, WV 26601–0085
304–765–2250
Statewide hot line: 800–352–6513

WISCONSIN COALITION AGAINST DOMESTIC VIOLENCE
1400 East Washington Avenue, Suite 232
Madison, WI 53703
608–255–0539 (local hot lines only)

WYOMING COALITION AGAINST DOMESTIC VIOLENCE
AND SEXUAL ASSAULT
341 East E Street
Suite 135A
Pinedale, WY 82601

307–367–4296 or 307–857–0102
Statewide hot line: 800–990–3877

U.S. VIRGIN ISLANDS

WOMEN'S RESOURCE CENTER
8 Kongens Gade
St. Thomas, VI 08802
809–776–3966
Islandwide hot line: 800–990–3877

WOMEN'S COALITION OF ST. CROIX
P.O. Box 2734
Christiansted
St. Croix, VI 00822
809–773–9272
Islandwide hot line: 800–990–3877

PUERTO RICO

COMISION PARA LOS ASUNTOS DE LA MUJER
Calle San Francisco 151–153
Viejo San Juan
San Juan, PR 00905
809–722–2907
Islandwide hot line: 800–990–3877; Español

National Domestic Violence Organizations and Other Services

The following is a list of nationwide domestic violence services:

NATIONAL DOMESTIC VIOLENCE HOT LINE
800–799–SAFE (7233)
800–787–3224 TDD

NATIONAL COALITION AGAINST DOMESTIC VIOLENCE
P.O. Box 18749
Denver, CO 80218
303–839–1852

FAMILY VIOLENCE PREVENTION FUND
383 Rhode Island Street, Suite 304
San Francisco, CA 94103–5133
415–252–8900

HEALTH RESOURCE CENTER ON DOMESTIC VIOLENCE
c/o Family Violence Prevention Fund
383 Rhode Island Street, Suite 304
San Francisco, CA 94103–5133
800–313–1310

NATIONAL RESOURCE CENTER ON DOMESTIC VIOLENCE
BATTERED WOMEN'S JUSTICE PROJECT
4032 Chicago Ave., South
Minneapolis, MN 55407
800–903–0111

AMERICAN BAR ASSOCIATION COMMISSION ON
DOMESTIC VIOLENCE
740 15th Street, N.W.
Washington, DC 20005–1009
202–662–1737

CENTER FOR THE PREVENTION OF SEXUAL AND
DOMESTIC VIOLENCE
1914 North 34th Street, Suite 105
Seattle, WA 98103
206–634–1903 or 206–634–0115

NATIONAL COALITION OF PHYSICIANS AGAINST FAMILY
VIOLENCE, DEPARTMENT OF MENTAL HEALTH
312–464–5066

THE COMMONWEALTH FUND COMMISSION ON
WOMEN'S HEALTH
Columbia University
College of Physicians and Surgeons
630 West 168th Street, P&S 2–463
New York, NY 10032
212–305–8118

THE CENTERS FOR DISEASE CONTROL AND
PREVENTION FAMILY AND INTIMATE VIOLENCE
PREVENTION TEAM
770–488–4410

THE NATIONAL WOMEN'S RESOURCE CENTER
800–354–8824

Elder Care

THE ELDER CARE LOCATOR
800–677–1116

THE NATIONAL CENTER ON ELDER ABUSE
202–682–2470

NATIONAL COMMITTEE FOR THE PREVENTION OF ELDER
ABUSE
c/o Institute on Aging
Medical Center of Central Massachusetts
119 Belmont Street
Worcester, MA 01605
508–793–6166

AMERICAN ASSOCIATION OF RETIRED PERSONS
WOMEN'S INITIATIVE
601 E Street, NW
Washington, D.C. 20049
202–434–2400

AARP/LEGAL COUNSEL FOR THE ELDERLY
601 E Street, NW
Washington, DC 20049
202–434–2120

NATIONAL BAR ASSOCIATION
BLACK, ELDERLY LEGAL ASSISTANCE PROJECT
1225 11th Street, NW
Washington, DC 20001
202–842–3900

AMERICAN BAR ASSOCIATION
COMMITTEE ON LEGAL PROBLEMS OF THE ELDERLY
1800 M Street, NW
Washington, DC 20036
202–331–2297

Ethnic Organizations

BIHA (BLACK, INDIAN, HISPANIC, AND ASIAN WOMEN
IN ACTION)
612–870–1193

MENDING THE SACRED HOOP, NATIONAL TRAINING
PROJECT
206 West Fourth Street
Duluth, MN 55806
218–722–2781

INDIAN LAW SUPPORT CENTER
Native American Rights Fund
1712 N Street, NW
Washington, DC 20036–2976

MIGRANT LEGAL ACTION PROGRAM
2020 S Street, NW, Suite 310
Washington, DC 20009
202–462–7744

NATIONAL IMMIGRATION CENTER
1636 W. Eighth Street, #215
Los Angeles, CA 90017
213–487–2531

Children

RESOURCE CENTER ON CHILD PROTECTION AND
CUSTODY
P.O. Box 8970
Reno, NV 89507
800–527–3223

NATIONAL COUNCIL ON CHILD ABUSE AND FAMILY
VIOLENCE
1155 Connecticut Avenue, NW
Suite 400
Washington, DC 20036
202–429–6695
National help line: 800–222–2000

COMMITTEE FOR MOTHER AND CHILD RIGHTS, INC.
210 Old Orchard Drive
Clearbrook, VA 22624
703 722–3652

FOR GUIDANCE WITH CUSTODY ISSUES

RESOURCE CENTER ON CHILD CUSTODY AND CHILD
PROTECTION
800–527–3223
 Information about child custody in the context of
domestic violence.

APPENDIX C

Books and Videos about Domestic Violence

Getting Free: You Can End Abuse and Take Back Your Life, by Ginny NiCarthy. Seal Press, 1982.

ETHNIC WOMEN
Chain Chain Change: For Black Women Dealing with Physical and Emotional Abuse, by Evelyn C. White. Seal Press, 1985.
Mejor Sola Que Mal Acompañada: For the Latina in an Abusive Relationship/ Para la Mujer Golpeada, by Myrna M. Zambrano (bilingual handbook). Seal Press, 1985.

You Don't Have to Take It! A Woman's Guide to Confronting Emotional Abuse at Work, by Ginny NiCarthy, Naomi Gottlieb, and Sandra Coffman. Seal Press, 1993.

CHILDREN

It's Not OK: Let's Talk About Domestic Violence. An eight-minute video produced by American Bar Association president Roberta Cooper Ramo and the Walt Disney Company. Ben Savage of ABC's *Boy Meets World* narrates the video, which tells kids domestic violence is not their fault, that there are things they can do, and that there are people who can help them.

When Mommy Got Hurt, written by Ilene Lee and Kathy Sylwester and illustrated by Carol Deach, is a simple, touching storybook for young children that answers many of the questions children have about domestic violence. Order by mail, $4.95 from Kidsrights, a comprehensive source for education and prevention materials in the fields of child abuse, divorce, domestic violence, drug abuse, stepfamilies, adoption, and family issues. Kidsrights, 10100 Park Cedar Drive, Charlotte, NC 28210, 800–892–KIDS (5437).

Mommy and Daddy Are Fighting: A Book for Children About Family Violence, by Susan Paris. Seal Press, 1986.

In Love and In Danger: A Teen's Guide to Breaking Free of Abusive Relationships, by Barrie Levy. Seal Press, 1993.

Dating Violence: Young Women in Danger, ed. by Barrie Levy. Seal Press, 1991.

INDEX

ABOUT THE AUTHOR

Marian Betancourt is coauthor of several books about women's health issues, including *What to Do if You Get Breast Cancer* (Little, Brown) and *Chronic Illness and the Family* (Adams). Two more books about cancer are soon to be published by John Wiley & Sons, and she is under contract for another book on women's health issues for Avon.

Betancourt has been a professional writer for more than twenty years. She is a member of the Authors Guild and is on the Executive Council of the American Society of Journalists and Authors. She was married to an abusive man in the days before domestic violence came out of the closet. The preface for this book recounts her personal experience.

She lives in Brooklyn.